General Editor: Aidan Chambers

THE
MACHINE-
GUNNERS

M Books is a series consisting of some of the best contemporary fiction for young people. Other books you may enjoy are:

Nobody's Family is Going to Change Louise Fitzhugh
The Slave Dancer Paula Fox
Elidor Alan Garner
The Owl Service Alan Garner
The Friends Rosa Guy
Slake's Limbo Felice Holman
The Nature of the Beast Janni Howker
The Vandal Ann Schlee
The Secret Diary of Adrian Mole Aged 13$\frac{3}{4}$ Sue Townsend
Lizzie's Floating Shop John Wain
Fireweed Jill Paton Walsh
The Pigman Paul Zindel
The Pigman's Legacy Paul Zindel
A Sporting Chance Aidan Chambers
Nightfall Joan Aiken
Loving You Loving Me Aidan Chambers
Ghosts Aidan and Nancy Chambers
Blitzcat Robert Westall
Love All Aidan Chambers
Eleanor Elizabeth Libby Gleeson

THE MACHINE GUNNERS

Robert Westall

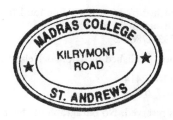

Nelson

Thomas Nelson and Sons Ltd
Nelson House   Mayfield Road
Walton-on-Thames   Surrey
KT12 5PL   UK

51 York Place
Edinburgh
EH1 3JD   UK

Thomas Nelson (Hong Kong) Ltd
Toppan Building 10/F
22A Westlands Road
Quarry Bay   Hong Kong

Thomas Nelson Australia
102 Dodds Street
South Melbourne
Victoria 3205   Australia

Nelson Canada
1120 Birchmount Road
Scarborough   Ontario
M1K 5G4   Canada

First published by Macmillan London Ltd
First published in *M Books* 1980
ISBN 0-333-27868-2

This edition published by Thomas Nelson and Sons Ltd 1992

ISBN 0-17-432414-6
NPN 9 8 7 6 5 4 3

Printed in Singapore.

To my mother and father
who *were* the mother and father of the book

ONE

WHEN Chas awakened, the air-raid shelter was silent. Grey winter light was creeping round the door-curtain. It could have been any time. His mother was gone, and the little brown attaché case with the insurance policies and bottle of brandy for emergencies. He could hear the milk-cart coming round the square. The all-clear must have gone.

He climbed out of the shelter scratching his head, and looked round carefully. Everything was just the same: same whistling milkman, same cart-horse. But there was too much milk on the cart and that was bad. Every extra bottle meant some family bombed-out during the night.

He trailed round to the kitchen door. His mother had the paraffin heater on and bread frying. It smelt safe. There were two more panes of glass out of the window, and his father had blocked the gaps with cardboard from a Nestle's Milk box. The lettering on the cardboard was the right way up. Father was fussy about things like that.

Father was sitting by the heater with his pint mug of tea. He looked weary, but still neat in his warden's uniform, with his beret tucked under his shoulder-strap.

'You remember that lass in the greengrocer's?'

'The ginger-haired one?' said his mother, still bending over the stove.

'Aye. A direct hit. They found half of her in the front garden and the other half right across the house.'

'She didn't believe in going down the shelter. She was always frightened of being buried alive.' From the way his mother hunched her shoulders, Chas could tell she was trying not to cry.

Chas's father turned to him.

7

'Your rabbits are all right. Chinny had some glass in her straw, but I shifted it. But there's six panes out of the greenhouse. If it goes on this way, there'll be no chrysanthemums for Christmas.'

'It won't be the same without chrysants,' said his mother. Her lips were tight together, but shaking slightly. 'Here's your breakfast.'

Chas cheered up. Two whole slices of fried bread and a roll of pale pink sausage-meat. It tasted queer, not at all like sausage before the war. But he was starting to like the queerness. He ate silently, listening to his parents. If he shut up, they soon forgot he was there. You heard much more interesting things if you didn't butt in.

'I thought we were a gonner last night, I really did. That dive bomber . . . I thought it was going to land on top of the shelter . . . Mrs Spalding had one of her turns.'

'It wasn't a dive bomber,' announced Father with authority. 'It had two engines. He came down on the rooftops 'cos one of the RAF lads was after him. Right on his tail. You could see his guns firing. And he got him. Crashed on the old laundry at Chirton. Full bomb load. I felt the heat on me face a mile away.' Mother's face froze.

'Nobody killed, love. That laundry's been empty for years. Just as well – there's not much left of it.'

Chas finished his last carefully-cut dice of fried bread and looked hopefully at his father.

'Can I go and see it?'

'Aye, you can go and look. But you won't find nowt but bricks. Everything just went.'

Mother looked doubtful. 'D'you think he should?'

'Let him go, lass. There's nowt left.'

'No unexploded bombs?'

'No, a quiet night really. Lots of our fighters up. That's why you didn't hear any guns.'

8

'Can I borrow your old shopping-basket?' said Chas.

'I suppose so. But don't lose it, and don't bring any of your old rubbish back in the house. Take it straight down the greenhouse.'

'What time's school?' said his father.

'Half-past ten. The raid went on after midnight.'

War had its compensations.

Chas had the second-best collection of war souvenirs in Garmouth. It was all a matter of knowing where to look. Silly kids looked on the pavements or in the gutters; as if anything *there* wasn't picked up straight away. The best places to look were where no one else would dream, like in the dry soil under privet hedges. You often found machine-gun bullets there, turned into little metal mushrooms as they hit the ground. Fools thought nothing could fall through a hedge.

As he walked, Chas's eyes were everywhere. At the corner of Marston Road, the pavement was burnt into a white patch a yard across. Incendiary bomb! The tailfin would be somewhere near – they normally bounced off hard when the bomb hit.

He retrieved the fin from a front garden and wiped it on his coat; a good one, not bent, the dark green paint not even chipped. But he had ten of those already.

Boddser Brown had fifteen. Boddser had the best collection of souvenirs in Garmouth. Everyone said so. There had been some doubt until Boddser found the nose-cone of a 3.7 inch anti-aircraft shell, and that settled it.

Chas sighed, and put the fin in his basket. A hundred tailfins couldn't equal a nose-cone.

He knew the old laundry would be no good even before he got there. He began finding bits of the plane, but they were only lumps of aluminium, black on the sides and shiny at the edges, crumpled like soggy paper. They were useless

9

as souvenirs – other kids just laughed and said you'd cut up your mother's tin kettle. Unless it was a piece that had a number on it, or a German word, or even … Chas sighed at the tightness in his chest … a real swastika. But *these* were just black and silver.

The scene of the crash was a complete catastrophe. It was the partial catastrophes that Chas found interesting – picture frames still hanging on exposed walls five storeys up; chimneys balanced on the verge of toppling – whereas the old laundry had been flattened as completely as if the council's demolition gang had done it. Just piles of brick and the bomber's two engines.

One engine was in the front garden of a council house that had its windows out and its ceiling down. The family were scurrying around like ants from a broken nest, making heaps of belongings they had salvaged, and then breaking up the heaps to make new heaps. Chas watched them as if they were ants, without sympathy, because they were a slummy kind of family; a great fat woman in carpet slippers and a horde of boys of assorted sizes; hair like lavatory brushes, coarse maroon jerseys that wouldn't fasten at the neck and boots with steel heelplates.

Chas went on staring over the garden wall. The woman paused in her doorway, a slopping handleless chamber-pot in her hand.

'Bugger off staring. Ghoul! Haven't you anything better to do?'

'Can I see the engine?' said Chas hopelessly.

'No. It's ours.'

'No it isn't – it belongs to the Air Ministry. By law.' Chas sounded confident, but his heart wasn't in it.

'No it don't. It's ours 'cos it knocked our house down. Bugger off or I'll set our Cuthbert on you.'

Cuthbert, the largest lavatory-brush, picked up a stone,

a sudden look of interest dawning on his face. The other lavatory-brushes closed round him in an offensive phalanx. Chas drew himself up for a parting shot.

'West Chirton rubbish,' he said, in a tone he had often heard his mother use.

'Balkwell snob. Go back where you came from. S'our engine. The newspaper's coming to take photos of us today.' She drew herself up, adjusting a lump of front door that stood propped against the wall. On it was chalked the legend BUSNES AS USUAL.

The first stone flew from the fist of a lavatory-brush. The phalanx began to move forward. Chas took to his heels.

The other engine was guarded by the local policeman, Fatty Hardy. He was wearing a white tin hat with P on it and looking important, but he was still the Fatty Hardy who had chased Chas off many a building-site before the War. Stupid.

This engine was much better than the one in the front garden. It still had its propeller. Though the blades were bent into horseshoes, the middle was unharmed, a lovely shiny egg-shape painted red. Chas nearly choked with greed. If he only had that ... that was better than any 3.7 inch nose-cone! The whole propeller was loose – it waggled when the wind blew. Chas's mouth actually filled with saliva, as if he could smell a pie cooking.

How could he get rid of Fatty Hardy? An unexploded bomb? Swiftly he bashed his eyes with his fists, throwing handfuls of dust into them until they began to stream with tears. Then he ran towards Fatty Hardy bawling incoherently. As he reached the policeman he put his hand up; school died hard.

'Please, sir, Mum says come quick. There's a deep hole in our garden and there's a ticking coming from it.'

Fatty looked distinctly worried. Airplane engines was airplane engines and needed protecting from thieving kids. But unexploded bombs was unexploded bombs.

'*Hurry* sir! There's little kids all round it, looking down the hole.'

Fatty grabbed his shoulders and shook him roughly.

'Where, where? Take me, take me!'

'Please, sir, no, sir. Mum says I mustn't go back there, in case it goes off. I've got to go to me gran's, sir. But the bomb's at 19, Marston Road.'

Fatty went off at a wobbling run, his gasmask case flogging his broad bottom. Before he was out of sight, Chas was at the engine. Its realness was overwhelming. There were German words on the cowling. *Öel* was the only one he could recognize. Everything was bigger close to. The twisted prop-blades curled into the air like palm-leaves. The red spinner, which he had thought as carryable as a rugby-ball, now seemed as big as a brewery-barrel. He tugged at it; it came off so far and then stuck. He heaved again at the shiny red newness. It still resisted.

'Nazi pigs!' he screamed, as his hand slipped and the blood came. He picked up a lump of brickwork, four bricks still cemented together, and, raising it above his head, flung it at the spinner. The beautiful red thing crushed in, but it still wouldn't budge. He hit it again. Another great white flaking dent appeared. It was a mess now, hardly worth having. But still it refused to come off.

There was a sudden roar of rage from behind. Fatty Hardy had returned, sweaty face working. Chas ran.

He wasn't greatly worried. Hardy was puffing already; he wouldn't last fifty yards. The only worry was the piles of rubble underfoot. If he fell, Hardy would have him. Placing his feet carefully, he ran towards the Wood.

The Wood was in the grounds of West Chirton Hall. At one time, his father said, the people at the Hall had owned everything. But then the factories came, and the council estate, and the owners of the Hall just curled up and died for shame. Now the house itself was just a hole in the ground lined with brick, and a black cinder floor. There was a big water-tank full of rusty water, and nothing else.

The Wood was bleak and ugly too. Grown-ups dumped rubbish round the outside, and kids climbed and broke the trees. But nobody went into the middle. Some said it was haunted, but Chas had never found anything there but a feeling of cold misery, which wasn't exciting like headless horsemen. Still, it was an oddly discouraging sort of place.

Each year the briars grew thicker; even Chas knew only one way through them. He took it now, wriggling under arches of briars as thick as your finger, interlaced like barbed wire. He was safe. Fatty Hardy couldn't even try to follow. He picked himself up quickly because the grass was soaking. The sky seemed even greyer through the bare branches, and he felt fed-up. Still, since he was here he might as well search for souvenirs. Chirton Hall was another place no one ever looked. He'd found his best bit of shrapnel there – a foot long, smooth and milled on the sides, but with jagged edges like bad teeth.

He sniffed. There was a foreign smell in the Wood ... like petrol and fireworks. Funny, it wasn't Guy Fawkes yet. Some kids must have been messing about. As he pressed on, the smell grew stronger. There must be an awful lot of petrol.

Something was blocking out the light through the branches. A new building; a secret army base; a new anti-aircraft gun? He couldn't quite see, except that it was black.

And then he saw, quiet clearly at the top, a swastika,

black outlined in white. He didn't know whether to run towards it or away. So he stayed stock-still, listening. Not a sound, except the buzzing of flies. The angry way they buzzed off dog-dirt when you waved your hand over it. It was late in the year for flies!

He moved forward again. It was so tall, like a house, and now it was dividing into four arms, at right-angles to each other...

He burst into the clearing. It was the tail of an aeroplane: the German bomber that had crashed on the laundry. At least, most of it had crashed on the laundry. The tail, breaking off in the air, had spun to earth like a sycamore seed. He'd read of that happening in books. He could also tell from books that this had been a Heinkel He 111.

Suddeny he felt very proud. He'd report the find, and be on the nine o'clock news. He could hear the newsreader's voice.

The mystery bomber shot down over Garmouth on the night of the 1st of November has been identified as a new and secret variation of the Heinkel He 111. It was found by a nearly-unknown schoolboy, Charles McGill of Garmouth High School ... sorry, I'll read that again, Form 3A at Garmouth High School. There is no doubt that but for the sharp eyes of this young man, several enemy secret weapons vital to the Blitzkreig would have remained undiscovered...

Chas sighed. If he reported it, they'd just come and take it away for scrap. Like when he'd taken that shiny new incendiary-bomb rack to the Warden's Post ... they'd not even said thank you.

And he wouldn't get in the news. It was a perfectly normal Heinkel 111, registration letters HX-L, with typical dorsal turret mounting one machine-gun...

Chas gulped. The machine-gun was still there, hanging from the turret, shiny and black.

14

TWO

CHAS reached up and tugged at the gun-barrel. One leg of its swivel had snapped with the impact. He wrenched at the other, but the aluminium of the aircraft body just bent without breaking. Besides, a belt of shining cartridges went from the gun back into the aircraft. It supported the gun like a sling against Chas's downward pulls. Perhaps if he loosened the cartridge-belt . . .

He grabbed the round barrel, put his plimsolls against the curving sides of the plane and went up like a monkey. He peered over the edge of the cockpit.

The gunner was sitting there, watching him. One hand, in a soft fur mitt, was stretched up as if to retrieve the gun; the other lay in his overalled lap. He wore the black leather flying-helmet of the Luftwaffe, and goggles. His right eye, pale grey, watched through the goggle-glass tolerantly and a little sadly. He looked a nice man, young.

The glass of the other goggle was gone. Its rim was thick with sticky red, and inside was a seething mass of flies, which rose and buzzed angrily at Chas's arrival, then sank back into the goggle again.

For a terrible moment, Chas thought the Nazi was alive, that the mitted hand would reach out and grab him. Then even worse, he knew he was dead. It was like that moment in a fight when you think you're winning, and then suddenly you're lying on the ground with your mouth full of salty blood and you know you're going to lose, so you start shaking all over. Only this was ten times worse.

He wanted to let go of the fuselage, drop off and run home. But something in his mind wouldn't let him; some-

15

thing found the dead man fascinating. Something made him reach out and touch the gloved hand. Inside the sheepskin, the fingers were hard as iron. The arm and whole body was stiff. The gunner moved, but only as a statue or a toy soldier would move, all in one piece. The flies rose and buzzed. Inside the goggle was a deep red hole full of what looked like ... Chas dropped and was violently sick against a little door marked *Nicht Anfassen*.

He thought his mother would be angry at him for having wasted a good breakfast when food was hard to get. Then he heard the nine-o'clock hooter. Everyone set their watches by the factory hooters. They went at seven and eight and twelve and five. But this one, a little silly warbly one, went at nine. Chas knew it well, because it told him if he was late for school.

School! School was half-past ten, and he had to get home and change into uniform. He must hurry. He scurried off through the brambles without a backward look.

But nightmares aren't so easily shaken off. On his way home he wiped the splashes of sick off his jerkin, but his mother noticed how pale he was.

'Look like you seen a ghost! What you been up to?'

'Nothing, Mum. Had to run all the way 'cos I was late and I've got a stitch.'

'Where's my basket?' Chas's jaw fell open. The basket was lying by the little door marked *Nicht Anfassen*.

'I forgot it. It's all right, I've hidden it in a safe place. I'll get it tonight after school.'

For an awful moment he thought she was going to drag him back for the basket there and then. She did things like that when she got into a temper. But she also had a dread of him being late for school, so she just said, 'See you do. You can't get a basket for love nor money these days. Your Dad bought that for me at Newcastle Market when we

16

were courting. Now get off to school before you get the stick.'

He sighed; she would never understand that you didn't *get* the stick for being late these days.

But even at school the nightmare persisted. Right through double-Maths and into English, usually his favourite subject, that goggled face kept on coming back. His hands turned shiny with sweat. It ran down his forehead. He never even heard the question Mr Liddell, the English master, asked him. Usually he was first with his hand up.

'What's the matter with you this morning, McGill? You ill?'

God, no. Being ill meant being sent home, answering questions, being sent to fetch that basket.

'Sorry, sir. Couldn't sleep in the shelter. Woman next door had kittens because she thought that bomber was diving on her personally.' The class roared.

The English master regarded Chas sharply for a moment, then decided to join in the laugh. Then he stifled a yawn and ran his hands through his greying hair. Mr Liddell doubled nights as Captain Liddell of the Garmouth Home Guard and found the experience wearing. Besides, McGill was a good pupil usually. But he had too vivid an imagination. A boy to like, but not a boy to trust.

Chas went back to his vision of the machine-gunner. For there was something else in the vision: the machine-gun, black, new, glistening. Even in his terror, *because* of his terror, he wanted that gun. He wanted to beat Boddser Brown. But how?

First, cut it free. His father's hacksaw should see to that. All his father's tools were wonderful, powerful, could cope with anything. But then he would need some way of moving

17

the gun. From the way it had swung on its mount he knew it would be heavy.

Cemetery Jones' bogie. That could do it. He had a vision of the bogie: a heavy two-inch plank with big pram-wheels at each end, and a soap-box for a body.

And Cemetery Jones was just the one who would go with him into Chirton Wood at dusk. Cemetery Jones was called after his father, who was also called Cemetery Jones. He was the keeper of Garmouth graveyard, and marched ahead of funerals in black gaiters and a top hat wrapped in black muslin, looking like the Devil leading sinners at a brisk pace to the Gates of Hell.

Off-duty he was very cheerful, with straw-coloured hair, pale blue eyes, some very grisly jokes and a laugh like a horse. He had gleaming wide-spaced teeth like marble tombstones, which he was said to clean six times every day.

Cemetery Junior had the same laugh, hair, eyes and teeth, though he didn't clean his at all, so they were very yellow. He said a dentist had once told him they were so widely-spaced they would never rot, and he was testing the theory out.

Chas caught Cem in school dinner. School dinner was a kind of self-discipline: the potatoes and the thin translucent custard tasted so queer that they required an effort of will to eat. But Chas had an uncle who was Chief Engineer on an oil-tanker in the Persian Gulf. Every so often, Uncle William was invited to a feast by the local sheikh, who would suddenly hand him a whole sheep's eye with grease-dripping fingers. If Uncle William could swallow it in one gulp without gagging, the oil would continue to flow. If not ... on such small things hung the fate of the Free World. Chas was training himself to be like Uncle William. He was even training himself to like the smell of burning rubber. 'It's an acquired taste,' he'd say to his friends airily.

18

Cemetery's approach to school dinner was different. He treated his plate as an artist treats his palette, whirling gravy, dried potato, dried peas and dried egg into cosmic whirls and brushwork, occasionally flipping a choice piece of impasto into his mouth. By the time all had collapsed into a grey soggy amorphous mass from which no further reaction could be derived, it was three-quarters eaten. This procedure he called the 'Potato Irrigation Scheme'.

'I've found something,' announced Chas mysteriously, over the ginger stodge. 'It's *Big*. I need your bogie to shift it.'

'Can't. Got my Guy on the bogie.'

'What you want a Guy for? No bonfires allowed this year. No fireworks in the shops. Nothing. You're potty.'

'I use the money I collect to buy sweets.'

'Look, it's just one night. This is Big – Bigger than anything you've ever seen.'

'Go on, you always say that.'

'Come and see for yourself, then.'

'When?'

'Tonight.'

'Got to do me homework before the raid starts. We've only got one candle in our shelter and Mum says it ruins your eyes.'

'Look, I'll give you an incendiary bomb fin, a real smasher, not a dent . . .'

'I'll come for the fin, then. But I don't believe the other.'

Chas's eyes suddenly glinted. He'd had one of his Famous Ideas.

'And bring your bogie with the Guy still on it.'

They were going down to West Chirton. Chas was on the bogie and Cem was pulling it, snorting and grunting like a horse. He always insisted on pulling the bogie, so he

19

never got a ride. When asked why, he always said he was 'getting his muscles up', but everyone knew he was really scared of letting go the towing-rope in case someone ran off with the bogie. People didn't grumble; they enjoyed the ride.

Suddenly there was the wild ringing of a bicycle bell behind.

'Oh hell,' said Chas and Cemetery together.

'Where are you kids going?' asked a bossy female voice. 'And why have you got two Guys on your bogie this year, Cemetery?'

'Oh, ha, ha,' said Chas in disgust. 'Faff off, Audrey Parton, we're busy.'

'*Busy*?' The scorn was finely done. 'Little things please little minds.'

'While bigger fools look on,' retorted Chas.

'In disgust.'

'At themselves.' It was an old boring routine, but Cem laughed like a horse. Audrey Parton rode past, and slewed round her bike to block the road.

'Tell me where you're going or I won't let you past.' There was something in the threat. She was bigger than either Cem or Chas: what Mrs McGill called a fine strapping lass. She had bulging hockey-muscles and grey ankle-socks, and red hair in pigtails and freckles. She fought boys and, alas, sometimes won.

On the other hand there were some good things about her, which made her the only girl Cem and Chas ever talked to. Her chest was quite flat, and she didn't giggle and whisper to other girls as you went past. She never told on you to her mother, and she was as good climbing trees and drainpipes as any boy. For a long time she'd led her own girls' gang, but now they'd all deserted her for sheer lisle stockings, ringlets, and mother's powder-puff. She'd become

20

a misfit. She said she'd always wanted to be a boy. She was the only girl who always had sticking-plasters on her knees.

Mrs McGill treated Audrey with respect, because her family were posh and owned a car. But Mr McGill said her father was skulking in a Reserved Occupation, making his fortune while better men went to fight for their country. When Mr McGill spoke in that sort of voice, nobody argued.

'Where are you going?' asked Audrey. 'Can I come?' Chas muttered under his breath a phrase he'd heard sailors use.

'Going to me auntie's at West Chirton,' said Cem.

'You haven't got an auntie at West Chirton.'

'Have, so!'

'Haven't, so!'

This went on for some time. Chas eyed her bulging muscles speculatively. That machine-gun was heavy. She might come in useful. Besides, the dead German would scare the little cow silly. She wouldn't interfere with men's business again.

'All right, you can come with us.'

'Lead on, MacDuff,' said Audrey, patting him on the head as the bogie rolled past. Chas felt his hair suddenly prickle, as if it was full of nits.

They hid Audrey's bike on the edge of the Wood and pushed in. They had to lay the Guy down to get the bogie through the briars. Chas thought that in the dusk he looked like a dead man.

He had to keep shushing Cem and Audrey. They both had fits of the giggles as they felt the tension.

'It's all just one of your stupid jokes,' said Cem, 'but it'll cost you that bomb-fin.'

'I'm not going to do any *dirty* things with you two in this

21

wood, so you needn't think I am,' said Audrey, caught between fear and desire. 'I don't mind kissing, but no more.'

'Eeurk!' said Cem. 'Who'd want to with *you*.'

Chas's chest was getting tighter and tighter. He was glad he wasn't alone. At least he'd get Mum's basket back.

When Cem saw the bomber, he laughed as if it was a joke.

'Shut up,' said Chas. 'There's a dead German inside. You can look if you want, but Audrey can't.'

Cem climbed up, dropped down again, and whistled. 'That's one for me dad.'

'No it's not. They don't bury them here.'

'Yes they do. Dad had a coffin full of ... bits, from this bomber at lunchtime. Well screwed down it was, I can tell you.'

'Go on, they send them all ...'

'Yeah?'

'To the War Office, to count them,' said Chas stoutly through chattering teeth.

'Is there really ...?' said Audrey, all eyes and woman for once.

Chas was not displeased with the effect he was having on her, but he said severely, 'Girls aren't allowed to look. They can't stand it.'

'Poor man,' said Audrey. 'He's a long way from home.'

'*Look,*' said Chas, 'we came for *this*.' He waggled the gun.

'Cor, you're not ... How can we get it off?'

'Got me dad's saw.' He pulled it out from under his jerkin. 'Hold the gun steady.'

He began to saw. It was hard work. He kept catching his knuckles on the rivets of the fuselage, and soon blisters came. When he handed over to Cem he'd cut a quarter of the way through the aluminium strut.

22

'Can't see where I've got to saw,' said Cem.

'I've got a torch.' The fuselage lit up, and the trees around. Chas couldn't resist a peep upwards, to see if the dead German was looking down, watching them.

When he took over the saw from Cem, they were half-way through.

'There's a funny smell,' said Audrey. 'What's that funny smell?'

'That's *him*,' said Cem, nodding towards the shadowy fuselage with a professional air. 'It gets worse as it goes along.'

'I want to go home,' said Audrey, beginning to sniff.

'Go then. There's probably other dead 'uns in the Wood, waiting to get you.' Audrey gave a little scream.

'Keep that torch straight. I knew a girl wouldn't be any *good*.'

'Oh, shut up.' But the torch-beam straightened and held steady.

'Put that LIGHT out!' The yell came from the edge of the Wood. Audrey screamed and dropped the torch. There was the sound of breaking glass and it went out.

'Oh God,' said Cem. 'That's Fatty Hardy. Shush.' But Chas went on sawing like a mad thing. He was nearly through that aluminium strut and he wasn't going to be cheated now.

He felt the strut give, and the gun fell agonisingly on his foot. He grabbed it up, and immediately it shook and leapt in his arms. A golden-red light filled the clearing, and a noise like Guy Fawkes gone mad. He let go of the gun, and the noise stopped. But he could see, where the aircraft tail bulked large against the sky, a great ragged hole had been torn in it.

A police whistle shrilled on the edge of the Wood.

'God, that's done it,' said Cem. 'Shall we run?'

But Chas sat hunched in a dream of power, remembering the vibration against his foot, the red sparks shooting up, and, beyond them, flights of dark bullets winging through the dark enemy sky.

'What we going to do?' whispered Cem frantically.

Abruptly, Chas returned to the present. Even shaking from head to foot, he was still the one who thought up the plan.

'What's your Guy's legs made of?'

'Sticks.'

'Get one out.'

'Whaffor?'

'We're putting the gun up it.'

The gun went, though it split the Guy's trousers. The old wellington boot just covered the end, though one of the Guy's legs was now inches longer than the other. Still, Guys were like that. Chas used all the string and wire in his pockets to make it secure, and stuffed the straw back into all the gaps.

'Right, out we go.' He didn't forget his mum's shopping basket.

They crawled through the briars towards Audrey's bike.

'Oh, lor!' groaned Cem.

Fatty Hardy was standing some yards off, staring straight at where they lay. He was accompanied by a warden, a woman in a headscarf, two small boys and a dog. It was the small boys who worried Chas, but it was the dog which barked and ran straight at them. Tears of rage filled Chas's eyes. To be so near to owning the gun and then . . .

The dog stopped two yards off and stood yapping hysterically. Chas threw a stick at it and missed. The dog retreated a yard and continued its din.

'Hey, that dog's found something!' shouted Fatty Hardy, advancing.

THREE

CHAS despaired. And then suddenly the night turned white, black, white, black, white. A great hammer banged on the dark tin tray of the sky, crushing their ear-drums again and again. Anti-aircraft guns. Then, in the following silence, came the noise of an aircraft engine.

Chug-chug-chug-chug.

'One of theirs,' whispered Cem. The dog whined and fled. Fatty Hardy shouted, and the whole group of by-standers were streaking away to the nearest shelter. Then that hammer was beating the sky again. Echoes of its blows rippled away, like someone slamming doors further and further off down a corridor.

Chas stared at the sky, trying to guess where the next white flashes would come from. They came in, in a scattered pattern moving west. Five at a time. That was the guns at the Castle. Then a group of three together. That was the guns at Willington Quay.

'What shall we do?' whispered Audrey.

'Take your bike and get to a shelter. We can manage without you.'

'But I shouldn't be out in the open during an air-raid.'

'You don't think these trees will shelter you from any-thing?' said Chas brutally. She went, wobbling wildly across the waste ground.

'What about us?' said Cem.

'I'm getting this gun home while the streets are empty. This air-raid's the best chance we got.'

'The wardens will stop us.'

'Not if we go by Bogie Lane.' Bogie Lane was a little-

used cinder track that led through the allotments to near home. 'No one'll think of looking there.'

'Right, come on then.'

The blackness of night was back. As they dragged and bounced through the dark, the warning note of the air-raid siren sounded.

'Dozey swine. Caught asleep as usual,' said Cem in disgust.

'It's a sneak raider. They glide in without engines.'

'And he's hit something.' Cem nodded to the west, where a rapidly growing yellow glare was lighting up the rooftops.

'Or else they got *him*. Must be Howdon way.'

'Only the one. All-clear will sound in a minute.'

But it didn't. They were halfway up Bogie Lane when the heard the *chug-chug-chug* of enemy engines again.

'More than one.'

'Six or seven.'

Ahead, the night lit up as if great blue floodlights had been switched on. Blue points of light hung motionless in the sky, brighter than stars.

'They're dropping parachute flares.'

The *chug-chug-chug* grew nearer. They felt like two small flies crawling across a white tablecloth. Up there, thought Chas, Nazi bomb-aimers were staring down through black goggles, teeth clenched, hands tight on bomb-release toggles, waiting for the cross-hairs of their bomb-sights to meet on Bogie Lane and the two flies who crawled there.

They dived for cover into a patch of winter broccoli. It smelt safe, because they had some in the vegetable rack at home. Chas envied the broccoli; because whatever happened, it would still be growing here tomorrow in the sane world of daylight, just ordinary. As ordinary as the Fry's Chocolate sign that the allotment-owner had used, upside down to mend a hole in his fence . . .

Chug-chug-chug. Overhead now. They were safe, because bombs always dropped in a curve in front of bombers. He had watched them fall in newsreels of the Polish Campaign, out of black Stukas...

Bang, bang, bang. The hammer was at it again, right overhead. This meant a new danger: falling shell-shrapnel. Chas could hear it, whispering and pattering down like steel rain all around.

'Go on!' screamed Chas. 'Get the bastards, kill the bastards!' Then silence, blackness, nothing. The parachute flares had gone out.

'Come on,' shouted Chas, dragging Cem to his feet. 'They'll be back in a minute.'

The bogie wheels crunched along the cinders, and they could hear the hard *knock, knock* of the machine-gun on the bogie's planks. They got back to the Square before trouble started again. A rough hand grabbed Chas's shoulder.

'Where the hell you been?' It was his father, wearing a tin hat. 'Your mother's worried sick.'

'She knew I was going down Chirton,' squawked Chas.

'Get down the shelter. Who's that with you?'

'Cem.'

'Get him down as well. I'll go and tell his mother he's safe.'

'What about the Guy?'

Mr McGill dragged the bogie roughly against the garden hedge. 'It'll have to take its chance.'

'Eeh, you had me worried sick,' said Mrs McGill, '*and* Mrs Spalding here, too.' Mrs Spalding nodded and sniffed. Her son Colin, in the bottom bunk, looked self-righteous. 'Her Colin never leaves her back garden at nights. He's a good lad. *And* I was cooking fish and chips when the siren went, and I had to turn the gas off and now they're ruined and I don't know what else we're going to have for supper because there's only dry bread in the house, *and* your father's supposed to be on night-shift and he can't get to work for the raid so we'll have no money, *and* I wonder that they don't pay him for being a warden, after all he works hard enough at it . . .'

Chas lay back on his bunk and let her words drift over his head. He was thinking about the machine-gun out there in the dark.

'. . . and leading Cyril off straying with you.' Cemetery's real name was Cyril, which was why he preferred being called Cemetery. 'I mean, leading Cyril astray like that . . . if anything had happened to him I could never have looked Mrs Jones in the face again.'

'Bairns shouldn't be let wander in the dark these days. Real wickedness, I call it,' said Mrs Spalding. Chas shot her a look of hate from the shadow of his bunk. She had fat knees in ginger stockings, which kept straying apart so he could see she was wearing apricot knickers. Her legs were mottled through sitting too close to the fire. His mother's legs, dangling over his head, had pinker stockings, and thank God she always kept her knees together.

They sat round, bleary-eyed in the dawn light. No more windows had been broken in the kitchen. The paraffin-heater and gas-stove were on again.

'I put Cem's bogie in the greenhouse,' said Mr McGill. 'By God it's a rare weight. What'd he make his Guy of, drainpipes?'

'Dunno,' said Chas, cutting his fried bread into careful cubes. 'I'll take it back tonight.'

'You can take it back this morning. No school today. The all-clear's still not gone.'

'Do you think it's safe?' asked Mrs McGill. Her husband looked out at the cloudless November sky.

'They'll not come again. Or the RAF lads at Acklington'll have something to say about it.'

'Is there much damage in the town?'

'Nothing. It was Howdon that copped it. They hit a gasmain and it's still burning.'

After breakfast, Chas crept down to the greenhouse with his father's spanner. The greenhouse had had a boiler and hot-water pipes for heating before the War, when coke was off the ration. Now it was drained dry, and Chas had found he could take the ends off the big fat hot-water pipes. The machine-gun could be slid down inside, if he could get those sticking-out drums off it. He fiddled with them carefully. He didn't want to blow the end out of his father's greenhouse.

He got them off in the end. One was full of live bullets and the other full of spent cartridge-cases. Chas hesitated. He'd have liked to have taken one or two bullets to school to show around. But ... once Fatty Hardy found that bomber's tail, he'd be round all the schools making enquiries, and there was always some kid who blabbed ... Better safe than sorry.

He wrapped the gun in cloth and slid it into the water-pipe without looking at it further. He screwed the end of the water-pipe back on. He hid the drums of bullets in the thick straw of Chinny's hutch. He'd just finished when his father came down.

'You pulling Cem's Guy to bits?'

Chas controlled a guilty start, and said casually, 'Just mending the leg.'

'You leave that to Cem. It's his Guy. I sometimes think you're a bit too free with other people's property. Got no sense of mine and thine, that's your trouble.'

Chas said humbly, 'Yes Dad.' Mr McGill cocked an

eyebrow at such humble obedience, but he soon wandered off to poke at his chrysanthemums.

For some reason, Fatty Hardy did not go back and find the bomber. Others did.

Two days later, Cem whispered to Chas in school assembly, 'Y'know those round things full of bullets? Got four more. They were clipped to the fuselage round the gunner's feet.'

'Where you got them?'

'Under some plant-pots in the shed. It's all right. Dad never goes there since the War – they're all cobwebs and chrysalises. Look at this one, it's live.'

Chas jumped an inch in the air. But it wasn't a brass bullet Cem held out inside his hymn-book. Only a black and yellow chrysalis. 'You can hear it tapping to get out.'

'Is the gunner still there?'

'Yeah. Phew, he don't half niff.'

'I don't know how you can stand it,' said Chas savagely. 'Ain't you got *no* feelings?'

'You get used to it. It's in the family. When my father went on an embalming course he saw one fellah eating his sandwiches, reading a book propped against a body.'

'Eeurk,' said Chas loudly.

'If you insist on talking in assembly, boy,' boomed the Head, 'you can have a little talk with my cane afterwards. Yes, you with the freckles in 3A. Yes, you, the one who's turning round to look behind him so innocently. Three of the best for you. Now, school, Hymn 235: *New every morning is the Love.*'

But getting the cane was not the worst. Two days later, Chas saw a crowd standing round Boddser Brown in the playground. They were all looking at something and laughing.

Chas hated Boddser; he had round spectacles and crop-ped hair like a German, and a great gangling grown-up body. He was stupid and a bully; an arm-twister who made his pleasure last a long time. One day last term he and his gang had held a kid's head down the toilet and flushed it three times. The kid nearly drowned and was off school for a week. Boddser got caned, but you might as well cane a rhinoceros. Chas sometimes dreamt of beating in his skull with an iron bar.

But he could never leave Boddser alone; he was so easy to take the mickey out of. And when he started to get rough you could always shout, 'Quick fists, slow wits,' or, 'Don't get worked up, you'll give yourself a heart attack'. Then everyone would laugh, because no one liked Boddser really. And Boddser was nearly as afraid of laughter as Chas was of Boddser's fists. Taking the mickey out of Boddser was like bullfighting; deadly but fun.

Chas walked across to the laughing group.

'Hey, what's up?'

'Hah, McGill,' said Boddser, 'King of the Incendiary Bombs.'

'Why don't you wear your nose-cone permanently – it would go with your spectacles.' There was a titter. Boddser flushed.

'Got something better than a nose-cone to wear. Look!' He dangled a black leather flying-helmet under Chas's nose.

Chas didn't have to guess it belonged to the German gunner. His nose told him. But he said calmly, 'Where'd you get that? Woolworth's?'

'Never you mind. That's genuine Nazi. And so's this money.' He showed a fistful of notes marked with Hitler's face and swastikas. 'And what about this? Mein Liebling, she's called.' He thrust out a photo of a blonde girl with pigtails. 'She won't be getting any more you-know-what for

31

a bit.' There was a brown trickle down one corner of the photograph. Chas broke out in a sweat and felt sick. Boddser had been through the dead man's pockets. Chas turned away abruptly and walked towards the cloakrooms.

'That's better than your rotten shrapnel!' shouted Boddser in triumph after him.

FOUR

'Mr Liddell!'

Stan Liddell turned back towards the Headmaster's door, wondering what he had done to bring *that* waspish tone into the Head's voice.

'Mr Liddell!' Henry Montgomery turned up his nose distastefully. 'We have a *policeman* in school, apparently wanting to see you. He hasn't seen fit to tell me his business. Top secret, apparently. Anyway, he has asked permission to use my study to interview you. Please see it's empty by the time I get back from break. I have parents coming.' He stalked away, black gown quivering with indignation.

Stan went in. There was a police-sergeant standing by the fireplace, staring at Henry Montgomery's imitation-marble bust of Shakespeare. As he turned, Stan saw he had a bad limp.

'Hello, sir!' It wasn't the way policemen say 'sir', it was the way a schoolboy says 'sir'. Familiar eyes stared out at Stan from an unfamiliar face: a face twisted by a scar that ran from chin to hair-line, and tight lines of pain round eyes and mouth.

'It's ... it's ... Green, isn't it?'

'Yessir!' The schoolboy grin was still there, though the man looked forty.

'But I thought you had a commission in the army?' Stan could have bitten his tongue off the next minute, remembering the limp and scar.

'I copped it at Dunkirk. They got me in the foot, the face and the nerves. So I was shovelled out as an invalid.

33

Still, I'm trying to make myself useful. Stops me remembering.'

'Sit down, won't you?' said Stan awkwardly.

'I'd like your advice, sir. We've found something . . . it's not pretty. The inspector's left it to me . . . we're short-handed. It's not really important and yet . . . it niggles me. Lying awake last night thinking about it, I remembered you, sir, and the way you always knew what to do when I was at school . . .'

'Anything I can do . . .' said Stan. He felt embarrassed.

'I'd like you to come and look at it, sir. As I said, it's not pretty, but I'd be grateful. I mean, well, you're in the Home Guard, so you'd know about weapons . . . and I think it's the work of boys. No one knows boys like you do . . .'

They drove from school in a police-car. Stan hadn't bothered to consult Henry Montgomery; if he didn't like it, he could lump it.

A way had been beaten into Chirton Wood at last, by the heavy boots of constables. One still remained on guard, looking queasy.

'We haven't touched anything yet, sir, though it'll have to be cleared up by tonight. And this is confidential . . . we don't want rumours spreading . . .'

The bomber's tail-section was still there, but changed. Every piece that could be twisted off for a souvenir had been. Bricks had smashed the last of the perspex, and caved in the aluminium sides. Someone had tried to set the whole thing on fire, and various obscenities had been scrawled on the black sides in chalk.

'Nasty, isn't it. And I don't think that's dog-dirt either.'

'That's not the smell of dog-dirt!'

'No, it was neighbours complaining about the smell that put us onto it. There's a dead man inside. I wouldn't look

34

if I was you, sir. Everything that's been done to the plane's been done to him as well, poor devil. I know they're the enemy, but really . . .' Sergeant Green was at a loss for words.

'Why I brought you here, sir . . . look at this.' He pointed to an aluminium spar still sticking out of the wreckage.

'Sawn through with a hacksaw,' said Stan.

'Now what would have been attached to that, sir?'

'Machine-gun, I suppose.'

'And there's ammunition missing, too. These planes carry 2000 spare rounds in the rear gun-position. I checked with R A F Acklington.'

'But who could have pinched them?'

'We thought it might be the I.R.A. at first. They've been pinching the odd rifle recently. But whoever heard of the I.R.A. this far north? Lancashire, yes, but . . . and look at that hacksaw-cut. Can you imagine a grown-up being that cack-handed? I reckon it's kids, sir.'

'Oh, surely . . .'

'What about that then, sir?' Green pointed to the bullet-holes in the rudder hanging overhead.

'Made by the fighter that shot him down.'

'Wrong calibre. They're 7.62 millimetre. The RAF use .303.'

'Then the gunner shot through his own tail in a panic!'

'The angle's impossible. Those holes were made when the machine-gun was already detached from the plane. One of my beat-bobbies actually heard it happen, the night after the plane was shot down.'

'Why didn't he investigate?'

'He didn't know what it was, and then the siren went. He thought it was part of the raid. I'm afraid he's not very bright.'

'You mean . . .'

'Some bright kid's got a gun and 2000 rounds of live

ammo. And that gun's no peashooter. It'll go through a brick wall at quarter of a mile.'

'Strewth!'

'And it's some really well-organized kid, too. Finding it, going home for the saw, getting the gun home through the streets and hiding it where his parents can't find it. That takes some planning. That's not a primary kid, sir, that's a grammar-school boy.'

'You can't mean one of *our* boys . . .'

Green gave a wry grin. 'I know them, sir, and you know them. Primary school kids can be tough and louts. But for real devilment give me a grammar-school boy gone wrong every time.'

'The Head's not going to like this.'

'He'll have to lump it. That's where you could help, sir.'

'Oh, *thanks.*'

'I wouldn't have asked, sir. But if they cut loose with that thing . . . they could kill twenty people without even knowing they'd done it.'

FIVE

'Ey,' said Cem, looking up from his potato irrigation scheme, 'there was a police sergeant in to see the Head this morning. He saw Liddell, too.'

'Trouble for some,' said Chas.

'Perhaps Liddell's pawned the Alderman Bewick Chronium-Plated Cup for Effort!'

'No such luck. Hey, do you think they're on to you-know-what?'

'The way Boddser's shooting off his mouth, it'll be any moment now. What about you going to Chirton Wood and having a check?'

'Aw, it'll be all right for today.'

'That's what Julius Caesar thought on the Ides of March.'

'D'you think I ought to go and have a look, honestly?'

'Yeah! Hey, Carrot-juice, can we borrow your bike this lunch-time?' He addressed a high-pitched scream to a very small first-year with ginger hair, across a dismal landscape of spilled water and melting, discarded peas.

'Cost ya,' said Carrot-juice, without stopping spooning in disgusting custard, his third helping.

'Two empty cartridge-cases, from a Spitfire?'

'Betcha picked them up on the Home Guard Rifle Range.'

'No I didn't. My cousin's an RAF gun-repairer. Cobber Kane gave them to him personally.'

'Cobber Kane's dead. He got shot down. Anybody knows *that*.'

'He gave them to my cousin the day he died.'

'Tripe, but I'll take them anyway, even if they are Home Guard.'

'Right.'

Cem pedalled off steadily on Carrot-juice's ancient Sunbeam Roadster. The saddle was so low that his knees seemed up round his ears. It felt a long, long way to Chirton Wood. When he got there he left the bike in a patch of stinging nettles, so that no one without gloves could pinch it. The wood looked deserted, but a great path had been carved in by rozzers' beetle-crushers. Cem knew he'd seen enough; knew he should go straight back to school, but he couldn't resist a peep.

'Gotcher!' Two large hands grabbed him from behind.

'Help, police, murder,' screamed Cem, and kicked and struggled, even though he knew the voice was Fatty Hardy's. He went on screaming until two passing housewives stopped to stare, and Hardy's face grew red with embarrassment.

'Sorry, constable, I thought you were the murderer.' Fatty Hardy hated being called constable.

'What murderer?'

'The one who did the girl in, in these woods. The Polish fellah.'

Fatty Hardy's face betrayed a trace of doubt. '*What* Polish fellah?'

'The soldier from the camp at Monkseaton, who strangled the WAAF here, Saturday night.

'Who told you that?'

'Woman in the chip-shop. That's why I came here, to look for clues. He done her in with her own silk stocking, didn't he? She was all blue in the face with her tongue sticking out.'

'Rubbish! Someone's been having you on.'

'What, no murder?'

'No, and push off before I run you in.'

'Yes, sir,' said Cem respectfully, and turned to the nettle-bed to retrieve the bike.

38

As he rode off, the look of triumph faded from Fatty Hardy's face. He'd forgotten to ask the one question he'd been specially told to ask.

'Hey, lad, come back. What's your name? Where d'you live? I have to have your name!' But Cem seemed to have turned stone deaf. Perhaps it was the effort of pedalling so hard.

Cem dropped into a neighbouring desk, puffing.

'They've found it.'

'Thought so. Watch it, here's Liddell.'

Stan Liddell swept in with his usual gusto, gown flowing and a too-short pullover displaying the bottoms of his braces. This suited Stan well, as he liked hooking his thumbs into his braces while he talked. He usually had something interesting to say, and today was no exception.

'Found this, this morning,' he announced, holding up the tailfin of an incendiary-bomb. The class craned and muttered.

'That's nowt, sir. Boddser Brown's got fifteen, and Mc-Gill's got ten.'

'Not like this one. See it's painted black instead of green, and has a yellow stripe? It's a new type the Jerries have just started to use. Twice as powerful.'

That caught their attention, and he held it for the next half-hour. Because he talked inside gen on weapons. He held up Home Guard training posters, diagrams of grenades and rifles. Then the talk turned to machine-guns, and alarm-bells began ringing in Chas's head.

You cunning sod, Liddell, he thought, and waited, un-screwing the top of his ink-bottle. There was one big poster lying still rolled up on the desk, and Chas knew what it was: a diagram of *the* machine-gun. Stan would hold it up, and throw his quick glance round the class, looking for the guilty face. Cem's face. There was no time to warn him.

As Stan held up the rolled poster with a flourish, Chas knocked over his bottle of ink.

'Oh, hell!' It went all over Cem's trousers. Everyone turned to look, including Cem. Stan's moment of truth was completely ruined. Chas mopped wildly with a hanky at Cem's trousers.

'That's a picture of *our* gun he's got. Watch your face.'

'For heaven's sake, McGill, will you pay attention! And you, Jones. This is a picture of a German aircraft machine-gun, the MG 15, calibre 7.62 mm, firing 1000 rounds a minute, effective range one mile.'

The class looked at him, but now they looked – not all innocent, but at least all equally disorganized. Stan knew he was beaten.

'Right, boys. Open your English exercise books. I want an essay on *War Souvenirs*.'

Silence fell, but for the scratch of pens. Chas knew how he could gain one hour, and no more. And that hour would be his last chance to save the gun. He stuck his tongue out of the corner of his mouth and wrote.

I used to have the best collection of war souvenirs in this town. I have eleven incendiary-bomb fins, twenty-six spent bullets, eighteen pieces of shrapnel, including one piece a foot long, and fifty empty cartridge-cases including ten in clips that my Dad's friend who is in the Armed Trawlers gave me.

But now my collection is second-best, because Boddser Brown in 3B has beaten me. He has a 3.7 inch nose-cone, and a pongy German flier's helmet, and lots of German money with Hitler's face on it, and a picture of a German girl in pigtails, called Mein Liebling. I wish I knew how he got these things, becos he's beating me hollow, and if I can't beat him soon, I shall have to give up and start collecting cigarette cards instead.

40

The bell went for the end of the lesson.

'Close your books and pass them up,' said Mr. Liddell. There was a storm of protest.

'But sir, we haven't finished. Can't we finish it for homework?'

'No, pass them up.' You could tell Mr Liddell couldn't wait to get his hand on those books. Chas grinned to himself. He owed Boddser Brown that one.

By four o'clock, Boddser was outside the Head's door, sweating. By five, he had been given six of the best. By half-past five, the police were at his mother's door with a search-warrant.

But long before half-past five, two dogged figures were trundling a Guy on a bogie through the foggy night, shouting 'Penny for the Guy!'

'Hey, we're making a fortune!' said Cem. 'But where are we going?'

'Quick, down Bogie Lane.' They angled the bogie into the narrow entry, and vanished from adult ken.

'But where can we hide it?' asked Cem.

'Bunty's Yard.' Bunty was a builder, but Bunty was now in the army, concreting pillboxes and stringing wire on the South Downs for the duration. Bunty's old dad came up some days to take care of the yard, but all he ever did was to sit in the cabin and get the stove going and brew tea. He liked talking to kids, because there was no one else to talk to. He let Chas and Cem poke round the yard, sometimes, providing they didn't break anything.

Bunty's Yard had a ten-foot brick wall, with jagged glass set in concrete on top; on three sides, that was. The side next to the railway line was just a rotten fence with two loose planks. It was these planks that Chas now pulled out. The bogie and its burden slid through.

'Where?'

'Into those old sewage pipes. Bottom one, in the middle.'

'Won't it get rusty?'

'What you think I brought these oily rags for?'

'Where'd you get 'em?'

'Me dad brings them home from work. Me mum uses them to light the fire.' The gun slid into its hiding place. Rags were stuffed up each end, and sand gently tossed against them.

Within ten minutes, plaintive voices could again be heard on the main street shouting.

'Penny for the Guy?'

As they approached Chas's house, they saw a black police-car standing outside.

'Ow!' said Cem. 'Scarper!'

'No,' said Chas, 'let's get it over with. Just remember, if you keep your mouth shut, and I do, no one will ever find that gun till Bunty comes back from the War.'

'Right!' said Cem, like a bulldog getting its teeth into a Nazi's shin.

Chas barged straight in, bold as brass.

'Hey, Dad, Cem and I made three bob with Penny for the Guy!'

His dad was standing by the fire looking pretty mad. Not with him, but with the police sergeant sitting on the settee. He had a funny sort of scar on his face. Mr Liddell was there as well, looking rather alarming in a captain's uniform.

Chas's dad didn't like policemen. He said they were officious gyets who would take the world off you if you let them; *and* half of them were crooks anyway. Besides, the police-car at the door would set the neighbours talking, and that had upset Mrs McGill, who stood in a corner compulsively wiping her hands on her apron. Anything that upset his wife made Mr McGill mad.

The police-sergeant now made things worse for himself.

'Penny for the Guy? That's Begging and Vagrancy. I could have you up in court for that!'

'Aye, you can take me to court as well, for that,' said Mr McGill. 'I had many a penny for the Guy when I was a lad. Didn't you, sergeant?'

'Let's get to business,' said Stan Liddell, uncomfortably. You could tell he knew the sergeant was playing it all wrong.

'You are Charles Harold McGill?' said the sergeant, in an ominous voice.

'No, he's Charlie Peace the Burglar,' said Dad, rudely. 'Cut the cackle and stop asking daft questions.'

'Please don't tell me how to run my business,' said the sergeant. Mr McGill turned and spat in the fire. The spittle hissed and danced on the black shiny grate. Heavens, his dad must be really mad to do that!

'Charles McGill, have you found any ... war souvenirs the last few days?' Chas pretended to rack his brains.

'Only a tailfin. Gave it to Cem, here. You got it, Cem?'

'Yeah.' Cem fumbled in his pocket and produced it, putting it on the table with a loud clink. The sergeant picked it up and looked at it a long time, then put it down again. He's doing that to try and scare us, thought Chas.

'Are you sure that's all?'

'Yeah.'

'Quite sure?'

'Yeah.'

'You were down West Chirton, the morning after that bomber crashed?'

'Yeah.'

'Why you looking so guilty, lad?' Chas hung his head.

43

'Weeell . . .?'

'I tried to pinch a nose-cone off an engine. Fatty . . . Constable Hardy chased me.'

'That all?'

'Yeah.'

'Where do you keep your souvenirs?'

'Down greenhouse.'

'Let's go and see, shall we?' They all went down the garden, with shaded torches. The rabbits blinked and bolted through their straw, in the sudden light. Chas remembered the bullet-magazine in Chinny's hutch, and closed his eyes in horror. He was glad it was dark.

'Let's see them!' They all came tumbling out of their roll of sacking.

'Hmm,' said the sergeant. 'I think these better come along with us.' It was a silly thing to say. Chas suddenly let himself go.

'But they're mine! I've been collecting them a year. All the kids have got them.'

'The nation needs scrap metal.' The sergeant went all pompous.

'But they're the second-best collection in Garmouth!'

'Let the bairn keep them, Sergeant,' said Mr McGill, a real edge coming into his voice. Chas could tell Mr Liddell was turning against the sergeant, too. But the sergeant blundered on. His crippled foot was giving him hell.

'All such things are the property of the Crown.'

'Tripe!' said Chas's dad.

'I think you'd better get this young man to bed, sir. He's getting quite hysterical.'

'Just like a bobby. Pinch all a kid's treasures and then blame him for crying.'

'Take him *away,* please. I'm afraid we're going to have to search your house and the whole garden, if need be.'

44

'Take the bairn to bed, Maggie,' said his father. 'I'm staying here. You can't trust bobbies.'

So Chas went to bed, while his father stood like an outraged colossus, watching the police dig up every part of his precious garden, dismantle his greenhouse heating system and break three panes of glass.

'Pity you haven't got anything better to do than ruining good plants and frightening rabbits.' The police went at last, frustrated and in a blazing temper.

'Be sure to let us know if anything turns up, sir.'

'Get lost!' said Mr McGill viciously. 'I'm going to the lawyers about you in the morning.'

It really was all very lucky. The police never dared open Chinny's hutch; besides, it was too small to hold a machinegun. What was even luckier was that Mr McGill never questioned Chas about the gun himself; he was the only one Chas could never have deceived. And if anyone ever again mentioned war souvenirs to Chas he only stormed on and on about dirty policemen, and who could blame him?

As for Stan Liddell, he walked off to the Home Guard HQ feeling an utter failure. The Home Guard HQ was in Billing's Mill.

Four hundred years ago, Mr Billing had built his windmill on the highest hill in Garmouth, to catch the best of the wind. By 1940, though, the sails, great wooden driveshaft and cogs had rotted to nothing. All that was left was a blackened shell of stone shaped like a milk-bottle, containing only a half-buried millstone, the buzz of flies and the occasional corpse of a cat.

Now, thanks to one Sandy Sanderson, it had a corrugated iron roof, new floor, and sandbags everywhere it should have sandbags. There was a lookout-post on top, with a telephone and a huge pair of binoculars salvaged from a wrecked Polish destroyer.

Whenever Stan Liddell felt miserable or a failure, he went for a talk to Sandy. Sandy was more solid even than Billing's Mill. He had appeared at the Drill Hall the day the appeal went out for Home Guard volunteers. Among the blazered schoolboys and pin-striped bank-managers he stood out like the Rock of Gibraltar. He was six-foot-four, broad as a house, immaculate in the blue uniform of a sergeant of the Coldstream Guards which smelt strongly of moth-balls.

Sandy had the air of coming out of moth-balls himself. Invalided out of the Guards in 1933 after 'some nonsense with a machine-gun', he had spent the last seven years moving from uniform to uniform. He had been a hotel porter, an A.A. patrolman, a cinema commissionaire; but none of them for long. His voice was too loud, his stare too fierce, his division of the world into gentleman-officers and barrackroom scrimshankers too simple. In civvy street, all too often, it was the scrimshankers who had the money and power.

That first day in the Drill Hall, Sandy walked in, glared round, and everyone fell silent. His eye fell on Stan and detected, beneath twenty years of schoolmasterly shabbiness, the bright young subaltern of 1918. He singled Stan out and drove him down to the far end of the hall, like a sheepdog picking out the ram from his flock.

Then Sandy's mouth gaped wide.

'Com-pan-eee 'shun!' Schoolboys and bank-managers leaped a foot in the air and stood transfixed. Sandy counted them and strode up to Stan, every step of his hobnailed boots as certain as a chime of Big Ben.

'Eighty-four men correct and accounted for, sar!'

All Stan could think of to say was:

46

'Carry on, Sergeant-major.'

Sandy did. Stan watched aghast as coalminers, accountants and errand-boys were arranged in size, numbered from the left, divided into platoons and sections. Sandy had an unerring eye for men. The local doctor was extracted, appointed M.O. and despatched to join Stan in the invisible Officers' Mess. First-World-War corporals were sniffed out, told to get haircuts and pull their socks up, and promoted sergeant.

When, half-an-hour later, the local army commander showed up, it was all over. The senior bank-manager, now a lance-corporal clerk, was writing down the names, religions and next-of-kin of C Platoon.

The army commander's face changed from worry to relief.

'See you've got things under control!'

'Erm, yes,' said Stan.

'I envy you your sarnt-major. Wish I had him. Can't beat the Guards.'

'Erm, no,' said Stan.

'Well, I'll leave you to it. Cheeroh!'

And so the Garmouth Home Guard was born. Since then, all Stan had done was to make two promotions (at Sandy's suggestion). And Sandy had 'won' a lot of stuff.

'Winning' was Sandy's word. Things the Home Guard needed simply appeared: sandbags, telephone, binoculars, mugs white china, wood, and an army van to carry them in. Stan never dared ask where anything came from.

When Billing's Mill was re-roofed, Sandy moved in. Stan never saw where he slept; but he was always there, and always busy: oiling rifles or whitewashing everything with layer upon layer of whitewash. In the middle of all 1940's gloom and despondency, Sandy was simply and profoundly happy. If Hitler came, he would die, as he had lived, in uniform.

47

He listened now while Stan poured out his troubles. Then he thought for a long time.

'Cheer up, sar. Your plan of attack was first rate. Quite obvious that copper mistimed his offensive. Didn't read the enemy's mind correctly, sar. Kids is cunning little beggars; just like new recruits. Can't turn your back a minute with them. But we'll outmanoeuvre them yet, sar. And if we got that gun ... I know just the place we could best use it ...'

'But it's not ours, Sarnt-major!'

'We could win it, sir, we could win it ...'

SIX

The next Wednesday evening started quite well. Mr McGill was on the two-till-ten shift, so there were only Chas and his mum for tea. But Cousin Gordon called, on leave again, bright in brass and airforce blue. He was carrying his rifle, because he had to be ready to Defend Britain Against Invasion at any time, and because Aunt Rose said she wouldn't have the great greasy murderous thing round *her* house while he was out.

He was just letting Chas play with it (with clips of dummy bullets) when the siren went.

'Get down the shelter, you two, while I put this sausage and chips onto plates. This is one meal Hitler's not spoiling.'

It was nearly as good as a picnic, scrambling down into the Anderson with knives and forks, teapot and plate of dried bread. Chas sat by the shelter door to eat his tea, staring at the garden path.

'If I was that beetle out there, I might be wiped out at any moment by a piece of shrapnel. But in here, I'm safe.' It had all the pleasure of standing dry in a doorway, watching the rain make everything else wet. He thought of the steel and earth above him, and felt deliciously safe eating his chips. He nodded at Cousin Gordon's rifle.

'Pity you didn't bring home something bigger. Then you and me could have had a go at the bombers when they come.'

'No need,' said Cousin Gordon, who liked playing the expert. 'You can shoot down a bomber with a rifle. We're trained for it. You have to aim a hand's breadth in front of them, to allow for their speed.'

'But bombers fly too high!'

'Don't you believe it. Most bombers fly at five thousand feet, which is a mile. This thing can kill at a mile.' He stroked his rifle.

'Can the . . . German guns fire that far?'

'Yeah, far further. Their Schmeissers can go right through the trunk of a tree.'

'What's a Schmeisser?'

'Machine-gun.'

Chas finished his chips thoughtfully, impaling five on his fork at once and then ramming the lot into his mouth.

'How often have I got to tell you?' said Mrs McGill. '*Cut* them before you put them in your mouth.'

Around ten, the all-clear went. Nothing had happened but two showers of rain, and long before the end, you could hear people standing chatting by their shelter doors.

'What a waste of time,' said Mrs McGill. 'I could have done the ironing. Goodnight, Gordon. Tell your mother I'll call on Friday.'

'Goodnight. I'd better get back while its quiet.'

They heard his boots clink away, and sat waiting for another clink of boots up the path, and the clicking of a pushed bicycle. Dad.

'Hello, love.' Mrs McGill kissed her grimy husband on the cheek. Chas had never seen his father come through the back door without his mother kissing him on the cheek. It must taste awfully sooty and oily. How much soot and oil she must have swallowed since she married him!

'Here's your supper, nice and hot.'

Mr McGill washed his hands but not his face. That came after eating. First things first. He didn't take his grimy boots off, either. Mrs McGill always put a copy of the *Daily Express* under his chair to save the carpet.

'Nice having the raid over early for once. I could do with a good night's sleep in me own bed.'

'Don't count your chickens. There's still a yellow alert on.'

'But the all-clear went!'

'That's the end of the red alert. The buggers are still hanging about somewhere. I think I'd better get me uniform on.' Mr McGill, foreman at the gasworks, knew such things.

'But your tea will be spoiled.'

'Put it back in the oven.'

Mrs McGill sniffed and picked up the *Daily Express* off the floor. Work-boots might never be cleaned, but ARP boots were always spotless and shining. Mr McGill, immaculate now, beret under shoulder strap, sat down again to eat.

Next moment, the lights went out. Then the cracks round the drawn black-out curtains lit up with successive streaks of light. Mr McGill's plate went crash on the floor.

'Oh those lovely sausages!' screamed his wife.

'Get down, hinny. Turn your face from the window. It's one of those sneak raiders.'

But it wasn't. Chas, lying face-down under the sofa heard the sound of many engines.

'Run for it!' They ran down the front passage and pulled open the front door. It was like day outside, there were so many parachute-flares falling. You could have seen a pin on the crazy-paving path to the shelter.

'The insurance policies!' screamed his mother, trying to turn back. His father stopped her bodily, and for a moment his parents wrestled like drunks in the front passage.

'Run, for God's sake,' panted his father.

The moment Chas set foot on the path outside, the bombs began to scream down. Chas thought his legs had stopped working for good; the black hole of the shelter door seemed to get further away instead of nearer. They said you never

51

hear the bomb that hit you, but how could they know? Only the dead knew that, like the girl who had worked in the greengrocer's. Chas saw the top half of her body, still obscenely weighing out potatoes . . .

Then he threw himself through the shelter door. He caught his knee on a corner of the bunk, and it was agony. Then his mother landed on top of him, knocking him flat, and he heard Dad's boots running, as he had never heard them before. Then a crack like thunder, and another and another and another and another. Great thunder-boots walking steadily towards them. The next would certainly crush them.

But the next never came; only the sound of bricks falling, like coalmen tipping coal into the cellar and glass breaking and breaking . . .

His father drew down the heavy tarpaulin over the shelter door, and his mother lit the little oil-lamp with her third trembling match. Then she lit the candle under a plant-pot that kept the shelter warm.

'Did you shut the front door, love?' she said to his father. 'I'm frightened someone'll nip in and steal those insurance-policies. And where's Mrs Spalding and Colin?'

Chug, chug, chug, chug.

'The buggers is coming again!' shouted Mr McGill. 'Where's the guns, where's the fighters?'

Above the chugging came a kind of rhythmic panting-screeching; and a kind of dragging-hopping, like a kangaroo in its death-throes. It was even more frightening than the chugging, and it came right up to the shelter-door. A body fell through. It was Mrs Spalding.

'Is she dead?' said Mrs McGill.

'No, but she's got her knickers round her ankles,' said Mr McGill.

'Aah had tey hop aal the way,' gasped Mrs Spalding. 'I

was on the outside lav and I couldn't finish. The buggers blew the lav door off, and they've hit the Rex Cinema as well. Is there a spot of brandy?'

'Aah pulled the chain, Mam. It flushed all right.' It was Colin, with a self-satisfied smirk on his face.

'You'll get the Victoria Cross for that,' said Chas with a wild giggle.

'Shut up, Charles. Have you got no feelings?' Mum turned to Mrs Spalding, who had crawled onto her bunk and was busy pulling up her knickers. 'I'm sorry, love. We got down the shelter so quick I left the brandy and the case behind. I'm worried about the insurance, too. Jack didn't shut the front door. Go back and get them, Jack!'

But the bombs had begun whining down again. Every time he heard one, Chas stared hard at the shelter wall. Mr McGill had painted it white, and set tiny bits of cork in the wet paint to absorb condensation. Chas would start to count inside his head. When the counting reached twenty, he would either be dead, or he would see little bits of cork fall off the shelter wall with the shock-wave, and know he had survived . . . till the next whistling started. It was a silly pointless game, with no real magic in it, but it stopped you wanting to scream . . .

His granda always said one only hit you if it had your name on it . . . he'd seen photographs of RAF blokes chalking names on their bombs . . . did the Germans do that too? . . . How would they know his name . . . did they have lists of everyone who lived in England . . .? Perhaps the Gestapo had . . . he must stop thinking like that, or he would scream . . . make a fool of himself like Mrs Spalding . . . play another game, quick.

Yes, there was another game. He was lying in a trench with Cem and Carrot-juice. The black machine-gun was in his hands, leaping, vibrating, spraying out orange fire at the black bombers. And he was hitting them every time. They were blowing up, it was their crews who were screaming now, being blown in half ... one, two, three, four, five, six, seven ... oh, this was a good game ... try as they might, the bombers could not reach him. He got them first, swept them away on the blast of the big black gun, sent them down into hell to burn ...

'Hey, cheer up, son. It might never happen.' It was his father's voice, and he was staring at the white, corky wall again, and for the moment, the bombs had stopped.

At dawn, they climbed out stiffly. They were surprised to see their house still standing; and the rest of the houses in the Square. And the next row, beyond the long back-gardens, quite untouched ... except two were simply gone. The ones on either side were windowless, had slates missing. But two were simply gone.

'Ronnie Boyce lives there ...' said Chas. He had given Ronnie Boyce a bloody nose two days ago.

'*Did* live there,' said his father. 'It was over quick. They can never have known what hit them ...' Fat Ronnie Boyce, with his shiny boots and mum with asthma ... where *was* he now? Up in Heaven? With a harp and a halo to go with his shiny boots? He hoped God wasn't too rough on him. He was a terrible thief, but probably being blown to bits was enough punishment for being a thief.

'Chas, lad,' said his father, very quiet. 'I'm going to see if Nana and Granda are all right. Most of the stuff that was dropped fell by the river last night. I want you to come with me ...'

Chas felt his stomach go heavy, as if he'd swallowed a cannon-ball. Not Nana and Granda too! He saw in his mind their neat house in Henry Street, with the white wheel for a gate, and the big white seashells in the garden, and the freshly-painted flagstaff where his granda ran up the Union Jack every morning and saluted it.

'Don't take the bairn, Jack,' said his mother, fingering her apron.

'He's going,' said his father grimly. 'He's fourteen now, and there might be errands to run, and clearing up to do.'

'He'd better wear his best suit, then . . .'

'Don't be daft, woman. It's not a funeral yet. He might get it ruined for nowt. Come on, son.'

They walked side by side down the road. Chas felt proud that his father needed him. It was a solemn occasion, a family occasion, an adult occasion. But his hands wouldn't stop shaking. He wondered how it would be. There might be Nana putting on the kettle, and Granda getting his morning coughing over. Everyone would tell bomb-stories.

Or there might be only a hole in the ground, like Ronnie Boyce's house. The whole world seemed broken in half. Nearby, the same old streets, women gossiping at doors, kids peering over walls. But above the familiar roof-tops billowed more smoke than he had ever seen: oily black smoke rolling over itself, trailing east to cover the rising sun, so that they walked from sunshine to shadow every minute. It looked like a photo Chas had seen of Dunkirk. In a way he liked the smoke-clouds; they were exciting. But was Nana's house making that smoke?

They turned into Church Lane. Blocked. Big red notices saying *Access Prohibited* and *Danger*. Policemen controlling traffic. Men pulling crowbars off the backs of lorries. A wriggling mass of white hosepipes, connected to hydrants that peed streams of water into the gutters like naughty boys.

At the far end of the street the red brick spire of Holy Saviour's was burning. Flames licked from every window from top to bottom, joining into a smoke-column that blew away east. Even the Germans across the North Sea would be smelling the burning this morning. And laughing.

His father was asking a policeman which streets to the lower town were open. The policeman was shaking his head. Chas watched the church. God lived there. If even God wasn't safe from Hitler, who was? Why didn't God *get* Hitler for what he was doing? Why didn't he send a thunderbolt on Berchtesgarten? Wasn't Hitler afraid to do such things to God? Chas had once spat on a church pew for a laugh, and walked in fear and trembling for a week afterwards. Where *was* God?

As he watched, the spire seemed to shimmer in the heat. It was shimmering more and more. It was twisting, like an outlaw shot in a Western – all that great brick height. It made Chas feel dizzy. Even a hundred yards away, he wanted to run. Great chunks of brickwork fell inwards into the church spire, like a jigsaw breaking up. The gilded weathercock on top tilted. Firemen were running in all directions. And then slowly, ever so slowly, the spire pounced downwards at the firemen, like a leaping red lion. It landed in the street and leapt forward again, with a mane of red brick-dust, grasping for those running legs.

One man fell as it touched him. Two of his comrades picked him up and ran dragging him, without stopping while the red lion still pursued.

And then it stopped, and Chas became aware of the rumbling and shouting. A group gathered round the fallen fireman, lifting him so his blackened face stared at the heavens. They forced some stuff from a little brown bottle down his throat. He began to walk about, doubled up, coughing.

'He's all right,' said Mr McGill. 'By God, he was lucky. He'll never be luckier. C'mon.' They walked to the next street.

'I watched Holy Saviour's being built, as a kid,' said Mr McGill.

'Will they build it again?'

'God knows.' But *did* God know?

The next street was empty, normal. Except for one policeman, and a notice saying *Unexploded Bomb*. There was a little hole halfway down the street, surrounded by the kind of red and white barriers workmen use when they lay drainpipes. A cat was sniffing at the little hole. Chas would have been worried about the cat, if he hadn't already been worrying about Nana.

'It'll have to take its chance, that cat,' said Mr McGill.

'I expect Saville Street will be open,' said Chas. It was the most important street in the town with no less than three toyshops.

But Saville Street no longer existed. It was just piles of bricks: the shops were piles of brick and the roadway was piles of brick. There was a green lorry at the near end, marked *Heavy Rescue*. A grimy man in a white tin hat marked R was sitting on the tailboard with a mug of tea. The mug was white and shiny, but it had black fingermarks all over it.

'How do, Geordie,' said his father, in a familiar sort of way. Heavens, the man was Uncle George, Cousin Gordon's father. His face was so black he looked like a nigger minstrel. Uncle George grimaced, showing perfect false teeth.

'By Gum,' he said, 'I thought I'd seen it all in the trenches in the Last Lot, but I've seen nowt like this morning. There's bits of bairns under that. We'll be three days before we get the last of them out.'

'How many dead?'

'Twenty-seven so far, and three out alive. We had to use our bare hands, brick by brick, we were that frightened

57

the whole lot would come down on top of us.' He pulled a sandwich out of a screw of greaseproof paper with those same bare hands and began to eat it. How could he be so heartless?

'Your family all right, George?'

'Aye, Rosie's gone to her mother's and young Gordon to his girlfriend's at Monkseaton.'

'Heard anything about Henry Street?'

'They had it bad. Taking the young 'un down are you?' He gave Chas a look. 'Tek care!'

He finished off his sandwich and licked his fingers. 'Rudyard Street's just about open now.'

Rudyard Street was no worse than what Chas was used to. Slates off, ceiling down, windows gone. Every second house carried that silly notice *Business as usual.* The photographer from the *Garmouth Evening Gazette* was busy.

The nearer they approached the corner of Henry Street, the more Chas's heart sank. Mr McGill walked faster and faster, like a man going to have a fight. His steel heelcaps rang louder and louder. Chas found it harder and harder to breathe.

They turned the corner. The wheel gate, the seashells, the flagpole were untouched. The Union Jack still flew. But the roof was a wooden, slateless skeleton, and sky showed through the bedroom windows.

'We'll knock at the front door,' said his dad. 'Stand beside me, and if I say shut your eyes, you bloody shut them quick. Understand?' Chas gulped and nodded. Mr McGill knocked.

Nana opened the door in her flowered pinafore.

'I knew you'd come. And the bairn! D'you see what Hitler and his Jarmans have done!' Her blue eyes were snapping with fury, her brawny arms folded on her large

58

bosom. She always called Hitler 'Hilter' and spoke about him as if he was a personal enemy, a sneaky-minded neighbour who did sneaky things like tipping refuse over your garden fence. 'If I could get hold of that bloody man I'd strangle him. He should've been strangled at birth. Snotty-nosed gyet. He's really done for your granda, y'know. He was going to brew some tea when it happened. It blew him all the way down the yard and split the back of his top-coat from top to bottom. The buggers couldn't kill him at Caparetto in 1918, but they've nigh done for him this time. It's a crying shame he's past it: twenty years ago he'd have seen the buggers off. Riff-raff. What's Hitler more than a house-painter, when all's said and done?'

All the time she was talking, Chas had the absurd fancy that Hitler and the Jarmans were sitting down to breakfast about two streets away, and that one attack by Nana and her famous rolling-pin would settle the war once and for all.

'Come in, if you can get,' said Nana.

Granda was sitting in his armchair, warming his hands on a mug of tea. He was wearing furry brown slippers, striped pyjamas, the split overcoat and a black beret with two highly polished brass badges on it. One was his old regimental badge, a lamb carrying a flag. The other was a German army badge, with the worn figure of a charging infantryman, and lettering no one could read. Granda pointed to that badge now.

'I knew I'd cop it last night. I dreamt *he* came back for his badge.'

He was an Austrian soldier whom Granda had killed in a bayonet-fight at Caparetto. Granda had taken the badge as a trophy; and ever since had dreams that the dead man came back and mutely asked for his possession. Granda had lived in terror of that man for twenty-five years, yet he could never be persuaded to throw the badge away.

There was a fire in the hearth, and the huge black kettle on it as usual. It began to boil now, and the lid began to rattle. Granda's teeth began to chatter and Nana took the kettle off quickly.

'That lid always reminds him of the machine-guns.'

But it was too late. Granda was lost in his old nightmare. His hand did strange things, pulled invisible levers, settled together in front of his chest as if he grasped the handles of some weapon. The index finger of his right hand tightened slowly on an invisible trigger, as his left eye closed, and his right squinted tight.

'*Range? Three-seven-five. Gun cocked. Two hundred rounds expended. Three boxes of ammo in reserve. Barrel cold, topped up with water. Spare barrel in reserve, half worn-out. Sir.*'

The family watched. Suddenly he braced himself, shuffling his feet as if groping for a hold. His body tensed, like a dog when it sees a rabbit, and then he began to shake all over, as if the invisible gun was leaping almost beyond control.

'He's badly,' said Nana. 'He hasn't done that for ten years. He thinks they're coming for him.'

'Oh my God!' screamed Granda. 'Breech is jammed. *Recock, discharge, recock.*' His hands moved frantically.

'I'll mix one of his powders,' said Nana. 'Come and give me a hand, Chas.'

They were kept busy at Nana's for the rest of the day. There was no hope for the house; the walls were cracked; even if the roof could have been put back on, the walls would have collapsed under the weight.

The most they could do was rescue all the bits and pieces – the glass paperweight with the view of Boulogne in 1898;

the great black Bible with the tarnished clasp; the bamboo table – and pack them up for storage. Granda dozed in his chair, the Battle of Caparetto fought and lost, his Kitchener moustache trailing over his open mouth. It was terribly black inside Granda's mouth. Chas was fascinated by it, kept staring at it, trying to see something in the blackness.

Had Granda fought his last battle? Would he die there and then among his bits and pieces? Sometimes his breathing went funny, but it always recovered. Sometimes he moved in his sleep. Chas was glad to go down to the corner shop for some more cardboard boxes. The corner shop was untouched; just fuller than usual.

Only once did he allow himself to slip away and look at Granda's special treasure. In the coal-shed – open to the sky now – on a nail in the wall behind the heaped coal, hung a helmet. It was thick with rust, and the twisted leather chin-strap was as hard as iron. But on top was a little bobble of candle-grease. In the dugout at Caparetto, Granda had used the helmet as a candle-stick. That was the original candle-grease – he had never removed it.

At three o'clock, men came with a van for the furniture. It was going, Dad said, to the Repository. Chas thought the word had a sinister sound, like Mortuary or Infirmary, but he didn't say so.

At ten past three, a taxi for Nana and Granda arrived at the end of the road. Nana and Granda were coming to live at the Square. Chas had lost his bedroom. He would sleep on the settee in the Front Room, with the mysteries of chiming clock, wedding photographs and moth-balls. He didn't mind. He was much more interested in that helmet. If no one remembered it...

Nana took a last look round her home.

'Pity about the coal in the coalhouse,' she said. 'Some trash will steal it. Ghouls.'

'You can't put coal into a Repository, hinny,' said Mr McGill crossly. He was tired, and had night-shift to look forward to. 'C'mon, that taxi's costing money. Come on, Chas.'

'Can I walk home? I want to see what's happened at the church.' His dad glanced at his watch. Two full hours to bomber time. He nodded.

'See you don't go near that unexploded bomb. And be home by five.'

'Yes, Dad.' The taxi drew away, leaving the house to looters and to Chas. The Union Jack still flew. He took it down, took it to the coalhouse, and wrapped his new treasure in it. Then he bounced along to Bunty's Yard skipping and mouthing Granda's remembered words.

Range three-seven-five. Cocked. Two hundred rounds expended ... The Germans were about to face a new Mc-Gill, with a new machine-gun.

'You're mad,' said Cem.

'No I'm not. We got Clogger now,' said Chas.

'Even with Clogger you're mad. There's usually ten of them.'

'Och, tripe!' said Clogger. He never said much of anything except 'Aye' or 'No' or 'Och, tripe', even to masters. He was very silent and very hard. He was the junior team scrum-half and had once played a whole match after losing two front teeth: spitting blood thoughtfully before putting the ball in the scrum, and scoring two tries.

He was down from Scotland to stay with his auntie for the Duration, because his mum was dead and his father in the Navy. If he'd wanted to throw his weight about he could have been the boss, a terror. But he was content to trail around after Chas because he liked his stupid jokes (and had actually been seen to *smile* at them twice). He had ginger hair and freckles, and always spat on his hands before he started any job, even a Maths exercise.

He knew about the gun, but he was safe. He never told anybody anything, even the time from his watch.

'Look,' said Chas, 'Sicky Nicky has something we need. We've got to make it worth his while.'

'Why do we have to build our camp in *his* garden?'

'Because it's in the right place. And because nobody ever goes there any more. Where else do you know that's *private*?'

Cem shrugged. He was beaten there.

'Right! So what do we offer Nicky? What does he need?'

'All right, so we walk home with him. And Boddser will kick your head in.'

'We'll see.' They were packing their schoolbags to go home. Across the classroom, alone as always, Nicky was packing his neat books, expensive drawing instruments into an expensive bag, nearly new. But all scuffed, mauled.

Nicky's time of ordeal had come. He looked pale, was already starting to pant. Outside, the wolf-pack was gathering: waiting to pull his bag from his hand, strew his books over the pavement, kick him when he bent down to pick them up, pour gravel down his shirt, pull his shoes off and throw them over walls. Not till Nicky was reduced to screaming blind hysterics would he be allowed to creep home weeping.

Every night it happened, regular as clockwork. The wolf-pack never tired of it. Mornings, they didn't bother. They were sleepy or had homework worries, or were late. But the end of the day was always rounded off by an hour of torture.

Chas looked at Nicky. The face was good-looking, with a pale girl's good looks. The hair was curly and kept long. He had an operation scar on the side of his neck. But did that explain the constant bullying? Every kid had *some* peculiarity – was fat or thin or had big ears. Chas got twitted because he had thick lips and a funny fold of skin on the back of his neck. So why was Nicky singled out?

Chas wondered how he himself felt about Nicky. He'd never touched him, but constantly teased him. Why? Chas shrugged. That wasn't the job in hand. The job was to see that, for once, Nicky got home unscathed. But not *too* painlessly. That would look suspicious.

Nicky sighed, closed his desk and walked to the classroom door. Chas, Cem and Clogger closed in round him.

'Good evening, Knickers, my dear chap,' started Chas. 'How seems the world to you today?' Nicky looked frightened and hopeful at the same time. Anything was better than the wolf-pack. They walked downstairs and into the yard, making remarks about Nicky's puny muscles; asking him how many times a day he went to the toilet, and whether he wiped his bottom with his left hand of his right. Nicky blushed, but it wasn't as bad as being hit with schoolbags.

The wolf-gang was waiting just beyond the school gate; nine of them, including pack-leader Boddser Brown. Chas kept up his flow of rudenesses, but watched Boddser out of the corner of his eye. Boddser was looking worried; he didn't like anything unusual.

'Gerraway, McGill; he's *ours*,' said Boddser.

'I beg your pardon, O Mighty One, O Star of the East, O Moon of my Delight. Your beauty is dazzling, especially your haircut, Four-eyes!' There was a titter even among the wolf-pack.

Boddser reddened. He looked uneasily at Clogger. He didn't like the new confidence in Chas's voice.

'Gerraway, McGill. I'm warning you. I've got no quarrel with you, for now.'

'Oh thank you, thank you, worshipful lord,' said Chas,

making low salaams. 'May Allah bless your luscious toe-nails.' The smaller group moved past the larger one. So far, so good. They went on down Hawkey's Lane, not hurrying. Hurrying would be fatal. The wolf-gang looked at Boddser. Already their victim was past any previous torture-place, getting nearer the main road where adults might interfere.

'Pull him out,' said Boddser to two of his minions. The minions dived for Nicky, who was between Chas and Cem.

Clogger moved like greased lightning. His steel toe-cap caught the first minion on the knee, leaving him writhing in the gutter. His fist caught the second full on the nose, drawing a satisfying stream of blood. The wolf-gang drew back, and looked pointedly at Boddser. It was up to him, now, and the main road, full of people who might telephone the school, was only forty yards away.

'Get past them,' shouted Boddser. The wolf-gang streamed past, well clear of Clogger's boots, and blocked the end of the lane, solid.

'Told you so,' said Cem ruefully. 'Bloody fool, Chas!' But he doubled his fists. He was loyal.

Boddser stepped out in front.

'Right, McGill, you've asked for this.' His bluster was gone. He had made up his mind, as a man might decide to nail up a fence he'd watched sagging all winter. Chas had made Boddser's dignity sag a bit lately; now it was to be mended with Chas's blood. Boddser didn't even sound cruel or gloating as he did when he tortured Nicky; just determined. The time for talk, Chas decided, was over. It was time for action. But what? Chas was quick, and not soft, but no one he knew could stand up long to the pounding of Boddser's fists, except perhaps Clogger, and it wasn't Clogger's fight.

He could dive, head down, for Boddser's midriff, slide down and pinion Boddser's legs and hope to push him over.

But that would end, inevitably, with Boddser sitting on his chest, banging his head against the pavement.

Boddser took off his gasmask haversack, then his school-bag, his school raincoat, his blazer. He rolled up his sleeves slowly, one after the other. Chas could think of nothing but to do likewise. He took off his gasmask case. It was not like Boddser's. It was a circular tin, twice the size of a large tin of beans and nearly as heavy. It swung from a long thin leather strap.

And then the idea came to Chas. It set him aghast. But it was maim or be maimed now. He put the case down carefully and took off his schoolbag and coat and blazer, laying them in the fine gravel of the gutter. He came up with his fists clenched, ready. Boddser advanced without hurry.

'Take your specs off,' shouted Chas. 'I don't want your mum complaining to me dad if I break them!'

'Playing for time, McGill,' jeered Boddser. 'That won't save you.' But he took off his spectacles and handed them to a minion, and advanced again. Chas saw the first blow coming, and ducked it.

Then he swung his right fist wildly, a yard from Bodd-ser's face, and opened his hand. Fine gravel sprayed into Boddser's eyes. There was no need for the second handful. The huge menacing figure was suddenly crouched up help-less, tears streaming down his face.

Calmly, full of murder, Chas picked up his gasmask case and swung it. It hit the side of Boddser's head with a sound like a splitting pumpkin. Boddser screamed but did not fall. Chas swung at him again. The gasmask case dented dra-matically. Boddser crashed into the corrugated-iron fence. Chas raised his tin a third time. All the hate of all the years, infant school, junior school, boiled up in him.

It was as well that Cem snatched the gasmask from his hand.

'You're bloody mad. Stop it, stop it!' Cem yelled. Chas snatched for his weapon again. Clogger kicked it away and held Chas's arms behind his back. Then everyone watched Boddser aghast as he reeled about, blood spurting from both hands held across his face. Then the wolf-gang turned and fled.

It was Clogger who approached the moaning lump, pulled the hands away and looked. A two-inch flap of forehead hung loose.

'Shut your wailing man; ye'll live,' he said to Boddser. 'Stop going on like a wee bairn.' He turned to the group. 'We'd better be getting him to the hospital.'

Fortunately it was only two hundred yards away. A stiff starched sister took over.

'How did this happen?' she said like a High Court judge.

'I hit him,' said Chas.

'What with?'

'Me gasmask.'

'You're a wicked, vicious boy,' said the Sister. 'I shall ring up your headmaster personally. You grammar-school boys should know better. You might have killed him.'

'He was bigger than me!'

'That's no excuse. British boys fight with their fists!' Chas felt like a criminal.

'British boys fight with their fists,' said Chas's dad, and went off to mend the greenhouse. He didn't speak to Chas for two whole days, and neither did his mother, even all through the air-raid.

'Britishers do not use weapons, they fight only with their fists,' said the headmaster, flexing his cane. 'Bend over, boy!' It was six of the best and very painful.

The class treated him with awe-struck and horrified

silence. It was their opinion that Boddser had asked for it, but Chas shouldn't have done it.

'But what do you *do* if you're small?' asked Chas hopelessly. Nobody answered; they got on with their classwork.

The neighbours said Chas was a wicked boy who would come to an evil end, mark their words. It was all very trying. Chas felt imprisoned in a glass bubble. No one would talk to him but Audrey. So it was Chas, Nicky and Audrey who started the whole thing off, one night after school.

'Look, there's Boddser,' said Audrey. Both Nicky and Chas jumped, for their different reasons. But Boddser was only getting on a bus to go home with his mum, his head still completely encased in a spotless white bandage that was changed every night. The school was beginning to call him 'The Sheikh of Araby' because it looked like a turban.

Boddser had come down in the world since the fight. For a start, his mother kept him off school a whole week; and then began calling at school for him every day at four o'clock in case the 'big rough boys' got him again. She went on and on to everyone who would listen about the amount of bullying that went on at Garmouth High School. But one or two people had told her a few home truths about her darling's arm-twisting, so it was doubtful if she even knew herself whether she was guarding Boddser from the World, or the World from Boddser.

But even discounting his mother's goings-on, Boddser was a flop. His gang didn't want to know him any more. There had been a disaster, and they wanted a new leader. Besides, now he knew what the other side of pain was like, he was uncertain of himself. He put out his tongue at Chas as the bus swept past, and fell to dreaming of future revenge.

'Sit up, you great hulk,' said his mother, poking him in the ribs with her elbow, 'and wipe your nose.'

Chas, Audrey and Nicky reached Nicky's gate and hung around, unwilling to break up. They were all outcasts now.

'Like to see my goldfish?' asked Nicky. 'It's six inches long.'

'Gerroff,' said Chas. 'They always die when they get too big for the jam-jar.'

'Tisn't in a jam-jar. He's got a pond all to himself. He's four years old.'

'And my pet rabbit's ninety-four,' retorted Chas, but without much heat. He was nosey, so he let himself be led in. They passed the Lodge at the entrance, with its windows boarded up and people's names chalked on the door.

'That's where Graham the gardener lives,' said Nicky, 'but he's gone to Birmingham to work on munitions.' The drive zig-zagged through thick damp rhododendrons, and ended up nearly where it had started. There was a great white front door, like a Greek temple, but the paint was peeling off it. A sailor sat on the steps cleaning his boots. They stared at him, but he just said, 'Faff off,' without looking up.

'We've got ratings billeted on us,' said Nicky. 'Come round to the kitchen. Might be something to eat.' They went in. There *was* something to eat: a loaf still warm and a seven pound tin of butter, opened and left lying like a tin of cheap peas. Nicky carved great lumps off the loaf. It bent like a concertina, and stayed bent. Chas stabbed into the deep well of butter. You could have got lost in it. Chas had never seen so much butter in one place since the War.

'Whereja gettit?'

'Oh, it comes off the destroyers. Everything comes off the destroyers.' Nick kicked at a mass of empty gin-bottles that lay stacked under the kitchen sink. Chas thought his mum wouldn't have liked that much. Or the plates of cold egg and bacon in the sink with cold water dripping on them, or the

69

half-glass of something brown with a dead fly in it. He suddenly felt sorry for Nicky; money wasn't everything.

'What does your mum do?'

'Not much since my father got killed.' Nicky's father had been a ship's captain. Before the War, Chas had often seen his ship steam in, with its great white hull and yellow funnels. Captain Nichol had always dressed in spotless white too, with yellow braid on his shoulders. Every time he came home, he gave parties and garden-parties, and Mrs McGill said that people who got invited really thought they were somebody.

Then, in January 1940, the *Cyclades* was hit by a German torpedo off Gibraltar, even though she was camouflaged with grey stripes, and smiling handsome Captain Nichol vanished beneath the waves for ever, and his photograph never appeared in the local paper again.

'Have some more,' said Nicky, pointing at the bread.

'Ta,' said Chas.

'What *are* you doing, Benjamin?' The new voice was haughty, but rather wobbly. A tall thin woman was standing in the doorway with a glass in her hand. Chas thought she looked like a film-star gone wrong. She was still wearing her dressing gown, though it was past four o'clock. There were stains down the front; they could have been tea or marmalade.

'What are you *doing*? Who are these *children*?' Mrs Nichol let go of the doorpost to come into the room, staggered, and changed her mind. Her dressing-gown was falling open and Chas thought she wasn't wearing much. He felt all queer.

'Fiona, what are *you* doing?' Another voice, a man's came from the room behind Mrs Nichol.

'That's the chap in charge of the ratings,' muttered Nicky. 'He lives here too.'

'Mind you behave yourself, Benjamin,' said Mrs Nichol vaguely, and drifted away. There was a long silence in the kitchen.

'Let's go and see the goldfish,' said Audrey abruptly.

They went down the long back garden. It was full of interesting things: walls and steps and statues, and queer marble pots on stands. Chas wondered if those were the pots where Mrs Nichol kept her money; his mum always said the Nichols had pots of money. But ivy was growing over everything.

They peered into the green depths of a large pool, and were rewarded by a flash of red-gold all of six inches long. Nicky sprinkled breadcrumbs onto the thick green water, and the fish rose, mouthing silently.

'There used to be twelve of them,' said Nicky. 'My father imported them from China, but this is the only one left. He's called Oscar.'

'Hello Oscar,' said Audrey softly.

'He only speaks Chinese,' said Chas. 'What's at the bottom of the garden?' There was a huge rockery, all overgrown with ivy, too, and the gravestones of cats and dogs. Nicky knew all their names, and talked about them as if they were still alive. The last, wooden, cross had no name on it.

'What's that one?' asked Chas.

'That's for my father,' said Nicky, and the other two looked away.

'What's over the fence?' said Chas at last, stammering. He climbed to the top of the rockery and peered over. And there it was – the view down to the bay and the sea; exactly the way any Germans would come.

'I vote we make a secret camp here in the rockery,' he said.

'Oh, yes, please,' said Audrey. Nicky nodded, after a

moment. They were his only friends, and he wanted to keep them.

'Where *you* bin?' asked his mother.

'Nichol's house.'

'You *what*?'

'I've been to Benny Nichol's house. He's got a goldfish six inches long, in a pool.'

Mr McGill set down the newspaper with its glaring headline *Invasion Imminent?* and took off his reading spectacles. 'What you been up to now?'

Chas's voice went up to a screech of righteous indignation. 'Nothing! I was walking home with him, and he said he'd got this fish, and I said he hadn't . . .'

'You are *not* to go there again. And you aren't to play with that Nichol boy again.'

'Why not?'

'Never mind why not. Because I damned well say not.'

'Look, tell me why? You always tell me why I can't do things.' His father looked at his mother, and his mother at his father. They both seemed acutely embarrassed.

'We can't tell you. You're too young to understand.'

'But it's a marvellous place to play . . .' Sensing their embarrassment, Chas pressed on unmercifully.

'You can play anywhere else if you like. But not at the Nichol's house, and that's final.' Mr McGill vanished again behind the *Daily Express*. Mrs McGill went on with her ironing. Chas knew a brick wall when he saw one. But he also had a taste for getting round brick walls. Nicky's house had suddenly become the most desirable place on earth.

'Oh damn,' said Audrey, 'I've split another fingernail.' She sucked and bit at her nail meditatively, looking up at

72

the sky. It was a fine sunset for December, with a rim of sun just showing over the trees to the west.

'I'll go and get some lemonade,' said Nicky. They watched him running and ducking towards the house, keeping out of sight of the sitting-room where his mother was, with the officer.

'He's not a bad kid when you get to know him,' said Chas.

'My mother doesn't like him,' said Audrey. 'She's told me not to come here.'

'Mine too.' Chas scuffed his foot. 'What's everyone got against the poor kid?'

'I think it's because his mother ... drinks.'

'So does my granda, but everybody likes him.'

'Well it's ... you know ... sailors.' Audrey blushed; Chas blushed.

'The barrage balloons are high tonight. Must be going to be a raid.'

'Go on, they only send them up that high to test their cables.'

They both looked up at the barrage balloons. There were five round the mouth of the river, each known to the locals by an affectionate nickname. There was the South Shields Sausage and the Willington Windbag. The nearest one was called the Fish Quay Buster. Their raising and lowering, by RAF men sweating at winches, was a regular treat for crowds of children; nearly as good as going to the cinema. For the adults, they were a kind of air-raid barometer, except that no one really knew what their raising and lowering meant.

At this time of night, the last of the sunlight caught them, long after the rest of the earth was dark. When they were very high, they glowed so small and bright it was impossible to tell them from the first stars. But they were not that high tonight. You could see their silver sides and fat fins; they looked like flabby silver elephants, nosing this way and that in the light breeze.

And then, and then ... Chas gasped. Black on the blue dusk from the east it came: black, twin-engined, propellers idling like fans, soundlessly gliding slow and low. A German aircraft.

A moan broke from Chas's lips; not of fear, but frustration.

'The gun!' But it was a mile away, in Bunty's Yard.

The plane drew nearer, lower. A faint sighing came from it, a whistling of strings and wires, like a kite. It was a fighter, with four cannon in the nose. The fighter wobbled, the nose veered and the tiny black cannon-mouths pointed straight at Chas. A face without goggles looked down at him from the cockpit, from rooftop height and only a football pitch away.

'Get down!' screamed Audrey.

'What's happening?' said Nicky, and dropped a whole tray of lemonade on the remains of the rockery.

But Chas stood, glaring at the pilot of the fighter. He was a Britisher! He didn't jump into holes like a rabbit for no German, even if he *had* four cannon. The German would laugh if he did, feel powerful.

'Nazi pig.' He stuck up two fingers in the air, and not Churchill's way either.

The pilot laughed. The plane filled the sky. And then there was an ear-splitting roar, and the air was full of black oily smoke.

I'm dead, thought Chas. I'm dead and I didn't feel a thing.

Then he started coughing and his eyes started streaming.

'I'm in Hell,' said Chas, and wasn't very surprised. But it seemed Audrey and Nicky were in Hell too, for there they were lying at his feet, coughing as well. And the smoke was thinning and there was the fence and...

74

The plane was nowhere to be seen.

'You fool,' said Audrey. 'He started up his engines. There he is.'

The black shape was streaking up river. The odd gun was firing now from the ships. Black roses blossomed round the plane, above, behind, never on target.

'Go on, get him,' screamed Chas. But the pilot was in a playful mood. He turned and looped, and spun his wings, like a boy showing off by riding a bicycle with no hands. By that time every gun had joined in. Tracers from the pom-poms on the Bank Top grew like red-hot stitches on the blue serge of the sky. But they were so *slow*, always too slow to catch the German. And then he was climbing, headed straight for the South Shields barrage balloon. The sound of his cannon fire came, thin as a zip-fastener, and a yellow rose grew among the black. The balloon was burning, falling, silver turning black, dropping off, like the paper on a French cigarette.

'Get that Nazi swine,' yelled Chas, jumping up and down. 'Are you blind? Get your eyes chaarked!' Men shouted that to the ref at football matches.

The fighter performed a beautiful half-loop, rolled over at the top of it, and made for the Willington Quay Windbag, which was being winched down as quickly as its frantic crew could turn the handles. The ack-ack gunners intensified their efforts.

'Oh Gawd,' screamed Chas, 'you couldn't hit a drunk in Guthrie's Bar of a Saturday night!' This was a phrase of his grandfather's that his mother didn't like.

It was at that moment that an over-enthusiastic anti-aircraft team scored a hit. On the Willington Windbag. It made a lovely bang that turned the fighter over on its back.

'Oh, no.' Chas beat a tree in agony. 'Where are those Spitfires from Acklington?'

The German recovered and made straight at them.

'What . . .?' Chas glanced up. The Fish Quay Buster, on its way down, was right overhead.

'Get *down!*' Audrey pulled him into the camp they had dug, a shallow pit three feet deep, with a wall of rocks a foot high round it. A week's striving, blisters, broken finger-nails, and it felt pathetic now.

The guns were following the fighter. The flashes were terrible, the shrapnel fell like black rain. Chas threw him-self across Audrey protectively. It was a man's duty.

Then the plane's cannons fired. The air stank with cordite. Shell fragments slashed through the trees and privet of Mrs Nichol's garden. With a roar, the Fish Quay Buster exploded. The stones of the rockery glowed brighter than day, and the burning balloon was falling right on them!

They huddled together in a final terror, pressed tight like kittens. Then there was a rustling, a last roar of engines dwindling.

They got up. The trees above them were full of silver, draped in festoons like a tent-roof. It was the remains of the Buster. It looked very large, and they were awed.

Then reality reasserted itself.

'Quick, grab some down. That stuff's waterproof. We'll need some for the camp.' As Chas climbed and hacked at it, the air-raid warning sounded, and three very angry Spitfires hurtled overhead. You could almost hear the pilots gnashing their teeth above the whine of their super-chargers.

They hid great pieces of the Fish Quay Buster in a dis-used potting shed.

'Good stuff, that,' said Chas. 'Waterproof. It'll roof in the Fortress lovely.'

'What fortress?' asked Audrey.

76

Chas pointed to the hole in the rockery. 'That will be our Fortress.'

'But it's hopeless,' said Audrey. 'We've worked for a week and it's only a little hole.'

'We need more help. It's time we buried our differences.'

'Not with Boddser?' said Nicky nervously.

'No, Cem and Clogger. We must work together for the common good.'

'Pompous ass,' said Audrey under her breath, but not so she could be heard. She *was* tired of digging in the rockery.

'Ey, Clogger,' whispered Boddser. 'Want to join my gang? Show you some dirty postcards my uncle got in Port Said.'

'Och, tripe,' said Clogger, and walked away. Boddser didn't follow him.

'Ey, Cem,' whispered Boddser. 'Want to see my uncle's postcards from Egypt?' Cem, who was rather attached to camels and pyramids, said yes. Boddser passed across a grubby pack of nude men and women in peculiar positions. Cem looked first incredulous, then embarrassed.

'Don't like that fellow's moustache,' he said, after thought.

Boddser changed tack.

'Glad you've broken off with that McGill. Would you like to come round one night and play with my railway?' Boddser's railway was much more highly thought of than his uncle's postcards, being British.

'I might,' said Cem, flattered. Then Boddser, over-eager, made his mistake.

'McGill's got that German machine-gun, hasn't he?' A look of disgust crossed Cem's face.

'Yeah. And two Matilda tanks behind his rabbit hutch

77

and a smelly pair of Hitler's underpants in his handkerchief drawer.'

Boddser retired in a deeply hurt silence to his French exercise; his back had the look of a hard-done-by man.

They'd all been hoping it would happen, but when it did, they were surprised. Chas and Cem were walking to school in the gloom of a December morning. As Garmouth High came into view, Cem gave his great guffaw.

'Cor, look at the new chimney!'

Chas, who had been carefully kicking a Bovril jar along the gutter, glanced up. A long thin aircraft tail was sticking up out of the school roof.

'Dornier Do 17,' said Chas automatically.

'Garn, it's a Junkers 88.'

' 'Tisn't.'

' 'Tis. Just look at those tailfins.' Cem pulled his aircraft recognition book out of his pocket. But the picture of the Junkers 88 had been worn away by long contact with conkers and toffees.

'Hey, there's Stan Liddell. Let's ask him.'

'Hello, McGill. After another machine-gun?' Chas let his mouth fall open in innocent amazement.

'What you mean, sir?'

'Skip it!'

'What is it, sir?' Chas pointed at the long thin tail.

'I'll tell you what it is. It's an early start to the Christmas Holiday as far as you're concerned.'

'No school, sir? It hasn't made a *very* big hole.'

'No, but its petrol tank's burst. The school's full of fumes. One accidental spark and up it goes.'

'Aren't we going to another school, sir?'

'No room. Chirton Junior copped it last night, and Priory Infants was flattened.'

They hung around. The others joined them, and there was the usual bomb gossip.

'A baby got born in our shelter last night,' said Audrey big-eyed.

'Congratulations, dear. What you going to call it? I didn't know you was expecting.' Audrey blushed to everyone's satisfaction.

'Me dad's busy,' said Cem. 'Some of the pensioners are dying in the shelters. Bronchitis, with the damp.' Everyone was reluctant to go home. It wasn't that they liked school, but it left a gap in their lives.

'Let's go and work on the Fortress,' suggested Chas hopefully. But everybody just groaned.

Two mornings later, they were in Nicky's garden; with school gone, what else was there to do?'

'Where's Chas?'

'He said he wouldn't be long,' said Cem. 'He's got a new idea for making the Fortress.'

'Bet it's like the old idea – shifting rocks.'

'Here we are then!' said Chas triumphantly, from behind them.

They turned, and drew back in a shocked huddle. There was an adult with Chas, a very large adult indeed, a man of about forty, strong and pot-bellied. They all knew him. He looked like a photograph of somebody's grandad taken forty years ago – blond hair clipped in the Prussian style and a big bushy Kitchener moustache. He wore an old-fashioned suit with waistcoat watch-and-chain, polished boots and a stiff collar. The perfect Victorian alderman, prosperous and proud.

'You fool, Chas,' said Clogger. 'Now ye've blown it.'

'No I've not. You know John's simple. He doesn't understand a word you say. He's just like an elephant, only not so bright. But feel his muscles!'

Clogger stepped forward and felt the bulging muscles. John smiled cherubically and said, 'Where you going now?'

'That's all he ever says – where you going now? Otherwise he just grunts.'

'How'd you get him to follow you?'

'He always helps the milkman give out his bottles. So I got an old milk-bottle and waved it at him, and he came.'

'Won't he be missed?'

'He lives with his mother, and she works all day.'

'What use will he be, if he can't understand what you say?'

'He'll imitate what you do – just try him.'

Clogger turned to the biggest rock in the rockery – a rock that had already broken two spades, and defied them for a week. He tugged at it, futilely. John bent down and grunted and the rock tore from its earthy bed.

'Here, John, here,' cried Chas, pointing at the place in the parapet where the rock was meant to go. John put it down exactly.

'Gosh,' said Cem, his face lighting up. 'He *is* as strong as an elephant. I just hope he never runs amuck.'

Mr McGill was tireder than any man should ever be. The Warden's Post had vanished under a direct hit and the fulltime sector-leader and his three phones with it. Mr McGill was now sector-leader, with one phone in the front of a boarded-up windowless house. In between, he kept the gasworks together 'with tin cans and bent wire'.

Chas hardly saw his father. The moment Mr McGill sat down, he simply fell asleep, even wearing his tin helmet. Often Mrs McGill would hurry to the kitchen to fetch his hot meal, only to return to find him face down on the tablecloth, snoring. Then she would hover piteously with the laden plate in her hands, wondering whether to wake him. Which did he need more, food or sleep?

Chas got used to a sleeping father in the room. He listened to ITMA on the radio, did extra French homework, to the sound of gentle snores.

Mr McGill gently stank. The last three times he had tried to bath, the siren had gone as he was undressing. Mrs McGill was terrified he would he injured or killed wearing dirty underpants. What shame it would bring on the family.

'I don't think you'd mind me getting killed, hinny, if me pants was clean.'

Mrs McGill was busy too; Granda had taken bronchitis badly and his cough dominated the house. When she wasn't nursing, she was walking miles from shop to shop, wheedling things out from under shopkeeper's counters: the odd bit of sausage, ten cigarettes here and ten cigarettes there. Neither insults nor stony silence deterred her desperate attempts to charm. Things were not easy between her and Nana; there were low mutterings about 'two women don't fit in one kitchen'.

So although Mr McGill sometimes stirred from his heavy slumbers to ask how the bairn was, or where he was, or what he was doing, nobody bothered much. Chas was in one piece, clean and cheerful, and came home promptly for meals. That was enough. It was quieter and easier for everyone when he was out of the house.

Cem's sister had a boyfriend home on leave. Andrew Morgan had a brand-new subaltern's pip, and twenty-four hours left in England before a darkened troopship carried him off God knew where, for God knew how long.

It was Saturday night, and for once a fire was lit in the Jones' front room. Cem Senior and his missus had tactfully gone to the National Savings Whist Drive. Andy had his tie unloosened, a glass of beer in one hand and the waist of the delectable Miss Jones in the other.

The only fly in the ointment was Cem Junior, who was sitting on the hearthrug, building towers of wooden blocks and knocking them down again. He hadn't played with the blocks for years; it was very irritating.

'Haven't you got any homework to do?'

'No school, so no homework.'

'Why don't you go and listen to the kitchen radio?'

'There's only a stupid play on – all love and kissing – yuk!' Cem kicked a block so hard it hit his sister on her silken shin.

'Cyril! You've laddered them and they're my last pair.' Miss Jones forgot her party manners enough to aim a clout at her brother's head.

'Steady!' said Andrew nervously. This could be his last chance to kiss a girl, perhaps for ever.

Miss Jones remembered herself.

'Why don't you just go off somewhere else?'

' 'Cos this is the only warm room in the house. I'm not going out in the cold so you two can ... anyway, Mum said I didn't have to.'

Andrew reached in his pocket for a half-crown.

'Fancy the pictures?'

'Nothing on but *love* films,' said Cem. His sister sniffed furiously.

'Isn't there anything you *want* to do?'

'Yeah, sit here with me blocks. Course, I could go to my bedroom and use these blocks to build a machine-gun emplacement for my model army – if only *somebody* would show me *how.*'

Andy sighed. He knew all about the designing of emplacements, being newly commissioned in the Durham

Light Infantry. But *that* pamphlet had been marked *Secret*. He hesitated. Miss Jones heaved her splendid bosom in indignation and that decided Andy. Drawing a child a gun-emplacement couldn't *possibly* harm the War Effort. He reached for Cem's French exercise book, temptingly laid near at hand with a sharpened pencil on top.

'Mind you make it *absolutely* authentic,' said Cem savagely.

'Yes, Constable Hardy?' said the police-sergeant with the scarred face, wearily. Who wasn't weary?

'It's a strange bit of nicking on my patch, Sarge. It don't make sense.'

'Well?'

'Someone's pinching sandbags, Sarge. The ones we tied to the lamp-posts for use against incendiary bombs. Somebody's emptying out the sand and taking them away.'

'But they're the ones dogs pee on! They're so smelly people won't even use them against incendiary bombs.'

'That's the point, Sarge,' said Fatty Hardy, triumphantly. 'No person in their right mind would pinch them. That leaves only one conclusion – it's the work of enemy agents. I wonder they don't just slash them, though.'

The sergeant leapt up, ignoring his crippled foot, pulled a lock of black hair over his right eye, stuck an ink-rubber under his nose, and gave the Nazi salute.

'To Hans der Ripper, an Iron Cross first class for demolishing von hundred and fifty Britischer Pig Sandbags. Heil Hitler.' He collapsed into his chair laughing hysterically. Fatty looked round nervously for a first-aid kit.

'Thank you, Hardy. That's the first good laugh I've had in weeks.'

'Darling?' said Mrs Nichol. She was standing staring out

of the bedrooom window in her négligé, looking wistful and smoking a cigarette.

'Yeah?' Commander Horsfall was lying on the bed, scratching his head.

'Someone's stolen our air-raid shelter.'

'Go on, I threw an empty fag-packet into it this morning.'

'Not *that* one. That's the one for the family. There was a much bigger one in the shrubbery, for the servants. Then they all got directed to war-work, so it was never used.'

'What's the problem, then?'

'Well, it's the principle of the thing. I mean, it was *ours*, even if we never used it. People seem to think they can do what they like with other people's property these days. Everyone's gone so immoral, and all they do is blame it on the War.'

'Come back to bed. I'm on duty in half-an-hour.'

'But I want to know where it's gone . . .'

'Sir?'

'Yes, Petty Officer?' Commander Horsfall paused on the house steps. The Petty Officer was the man Audrey and Chas had seen cleaning his boots there, the first day.

'There's some thieving going on, sir.'

'That from you, Petty Officer Robinson, is pretty rich. You mean someone's been thieving from you, for a change?'

'Yessir.'

'What's missing?'

'Three tin hats; two fire-buckets; one notice-board; one stove, paraffin, heating; and one pump, stirrup.'

'Hardly the Black Market gang's line, are they, Petty Officer? Now seven-pound tins of butter . . .' Robinson had the grace to blush.

'Reckon it's that kid, sir . . . hers . . . sly little devil.'

Horsfall frowned. The last thing he wanted was trouble with that kid.

'We don't want bother, sir, do we, sir? Far too snug we are here, sir.'

Horsfall nodded. 'Make out a requisition for new ones. Say the old ones fell overboard. I'll sign it.'

'I'll help you with that concreting, Dad,' said Chas. It was a bright Sunday morning after a bombless night, and Mr McGill felt like doing a bit in the garden. But he still looked up suspiciously.

'Help me? You feeling all right? What's the matter – all your little friends gone to church?'

'No,' said Chas at his most innocent, 'I just felt like helping. I want to see how you do it.'

'Well,' said Mr McGill, 'you won't see much. Some thieving gyet's pinched half me cement. You wouldn't know anything about that?'

'No, Dad,' said Chas.

SEVEN

It was Christmas Eve and getting dark, with quick flurries of snow on the east wind. Chas and Clogger were in the Crow's Nest. Chas was wearing his suede jerkin and a bright red steel helmet marked *Caparetto* in fairly-neat white lettering. Clogger was wearing his boy scout uniform and another bright red helmet, also marked *Caparetto*.

Chas was very uncomfortable; the wind made his eyes water, and the iron-hard chin-strap of the old helmet was cutting into his chin.

The Crow's Nest was well made of Royal Navy packing-cases and perched in the highest tree. It had a roof of Fish Quay Buster, that rippled like thunder in the wind.

Clogger swept the horizon again, with the great brass telescope that had belonged to Captain Nichol.

'Nothing in sight, sir. He'll no come tonight. Visibility's down to a hundred yards and ma auntie'll be mad if A'm not home for tea soon.'

'O.K. Stand down, Petty Officer.' They climbed stiffly down the rope ladder, manhandling the telescope between them, and wriggled into Fortress Caparetto. It was great in the Fortress. The Quartermaster-cook had the kettle nearly boiling on the paraffin-heater, and the long Anderson shelter was as warm as toast. You could *make* toast on the paraffin-heater, if you were patient enough. It took half-an-hour, and it was hard to tell if the dark patches were toasting or soot; but it tasted hot and fine, spread with plenty of butter from the seven-pound tin. Clogger said the tin of butter would keep for ages in this cold weather.

Sergeant Jones, Private Nichol and Corporal Carstairs

(otherwise known as Carrot-juice) lounged on the pink-sprigged mattresses that covered the bunks, staring at the candle-flames and waiting for their brew, as content as cats. There was nowhere as safe as Fortress Caparetto in the whole of Garmouth. Above the thin steel of the Anderson's arched roof were three solid feet of earth and rockery, con-creted together here and there. It would have withstood anything but a direct hit from the *Bismarck*. An old patch-work quilt kept draughts from the door. Beyond, lay the machine-gun emplacement, walled with pongy sandbags and floored with a framework of boards.

Chas's heart glowed with pride. All done in a fortnight and as dry as a bone, thanks to the Fish Quay Buster. And the Quartermaster, she kept it so *neat* with rows of shining white mugs, red firebuckets brimming with sand, red hel-mets hanging on the wall and a notice-board marked *Fortress Caparetto – Standing Orders*. Chas was not quite sure what Standing Orders were, so they were read out twice a day, with everybody standing up respectfully.

1. Anyone who steals food from the Fortress, if found guilty by Court Martial, shall be thrown in the goldfish pond. They may take off any clothes they want to first, but Keep It Decent.
2. Anyone touching the Gun without permission will be chucked out of the Fortress for Three Months. Anyone who speaks to Boddser Brown for any reason will be chucked out for Good.
3. Anyone lying on the bunks will tidy up afterwards.
4. No peeing within fifty yards, or Anything Else.
5. Always come in by the back fence, after making sure you're not followed.
6. No stealing from shops without permission. All goods stolen belong to the Fortress.
7. Only sentries will touch the air-rifle. Hand back all pellets out of your pockets etc when coming off duty.
8. Do not mess about with catapults inside the Fortress or you will wash up for four days.

9. Do not mess about at all.

10. Penalty for splitting to parents, teachers etc is **DEATH**.

11. Do not waste anything.

12. Anyone who brings in useless old junk will take it back to the Tip where they got it.

13. Quartermaster gives out all the eats. Don't argue with her.

After the orders had been read out, everyone bent and swore to keep them, with their hands on the machine-gun.

John sat in the seat of honour, the only armchair. He was always given the first cup of tea and the first piece of toast. After all, it was John who had made it all possible. Chas's scheme had worked very well. John had come willingly, enjoying the change from milk-bottles. And he was a good imitator; you didn't have to show him any job twice.

It was just that he was so very strong; sometimes, when he got an idea wrong, he was impossible to stop. Once he had carried a great section of Anderson shelter right past the windows of Mrs Nichol's bedroom. But somehow she hadn't heard or looked. And the whole gang, heaving and straining, had pulled John back on course.

But that had been the early days. Now the children could handle him firmly and precisely, as a good mahout handles a good elephant.

Only now Fortress Caparetto was finished. There was no more work for him to do; and he did take up a lot of space.

'Where you going now?' he said, slurping his tea noisily.

'What are we going to *do* with him?' whispered Cem.

'Just not fetch him any more,' said Chas. 'He's not bright enough to find his way here by himself.'

'I hope you're right,' said Cem.

So, as the night fell, they took John home for what they thought was the last time.

Nicky wakened with a start. He switched on his bed-side light. His alarm-clock said half-past-one. Why had he wakened? He slept till morning usually; sleep was a refuge.

Was it bombers coming? He listened. The night was silent. He got up to go to the toilet.

As he passed his mother's door he saw her light was still on, and heard her voice, low and whispering, laughing. Then that man's voice. He was in there again. Nicky stood, his fist clenched. He hated that man. He would like to rush in and kill him, but he was only Sicky Nicky, puny, puny, puny. Tears started in his eyes and he fled to the toilet. Sitting on it, he began wondering again what had wakened him.

But he could think of nothing; only there had been the smell of the sea in his bedroom, as there was some nights when the wind was in the east. The wind carried the sound of the fog-horn too.

When his father had been alive, and at sea, Nicky had liked that smell of the sea, and the sound of the foghorn. It made him imagine the bridge of the *Cyclades* lit by the dim lights of the compass binnacle and chart-table; and his father's face, keen, commanding, bringing the great ship home through the dark. He had felt close to his father.

But now the smell of the sea and the sound of the horn were a desolation.

He tiptoed back past the hated door and slept again. And again he awakened, to the smell of the sea.

He tiptoed right round the house. Sailors snored behind doors. In the kitchen, mice scattered from view as the light went on. He put the light out again and lifted a corner of the blackout curtain. Stars and silence; the fog must be clearing from the harbour mouth. The horn had stopped.

But now the fear was in him. Something terrible was going to happen. He must run. But where?

Beneath the stars he could see the trees where the Crow's Nest was. The Fortress; that's where he must run to. Quickly now. The danger was near. He snatched up clothes, shoes, a torch and his teddy-bear and ran.

'Dead in their bed of sin they was,' said Mrs Spalding dramatically, waggling the curling-pins under her head-scarf. 'And a Judgement I call it. Lying there without a stitch on, nor a mark on their bodies. It was the Blast what done it. Or the Hand of God. God is not mocked!'

'Not in front of the bairn please, Mrs Spalding,' said Chas's father, putting down his knife and fork with an ominous clink. But not sufficiently ominous to stop Mrs Spalding in full cry.

'But that bairn, that poor little bairn who never did any harm. Why did God take *him*?' She raised her finger to the cracked ceiling, as if the Almighty were perched on the lampshade like a pet budgie.

'Mrs Spalding!' thundered Mr McGill.

'The bomb fell right on his little room where he was lying innocent asleep. They found not one little piece of him. He's with the angels now.'

Chas had an absurd picture of angels piecing together some unknown innocent's arms and legs, as if he was a jig-saw puzzle. Mr McGill looked at Chas, and jerked his head.

'Out!' Chas fled; as far as the keyhole of the kitchen door. He listened intently. Mrs Spalding said:

'You needn't look at me like that, Mr McGill. I'm doing no more than speaking the truth. There's been sin and wickedness in that house ever since Captain Nichol was lost, God rest his soul.'

Chas felt sick. Nicky's house had been bombed. Nicky,

his mother and that naval officer all dead. Oh, lord, the Fortress! The machine-gun!

'And all them pore sailor-boys stiff and stark,' intoned Mrs Spalding. Chas ran like the wind.

The Nichol house looked almost normal. The bomb had hit at the back, and the front retained its roof, and even some windows. Police, wardens, heavy rescue and ambulance had departed. Someone had closed the front gates and wired them together.

The garden wall was high, with spikes on top. Chas looked round furtively and climbed over the wired gate. He skirted the house and went into the back garden. The overgrown lawn was strewn with bricks and tiles; where Nick's bedroom had once been there was a brick-red gash. Chas couldn't see any blood-splashes.

Further on, statues and garden-urns lay toppled. The goldfish pond had cracked and was empty. One dead goldfish lay on the frozen weed at the bottom. The tiny stream that had fed the pool was spreading across the whole garden, turning it into a swamp and then freezing.

The Crow's Nest was still there, though thrown askew by the blast. Well, that could be rebuilt. The Fortress ... they had built well. There was not a sandbag out of place.

Chas pulled back the old quilt and went in.

His skin crept; there was something alive with him in the dark. An odd voice said:

'Chas?'

'Nicky! How did you escape?'

'My father came in a dream and warned me.'

'Oh.'

'They're all dead. Even the ratings.'

'Oh.'

'I went back and found them.'

'Oh. What'll you do now?'

There was a long pause. 'I don't know. There's no one else in our family. I suppose they'll put me in a home.'

'Hard luck. I wish you could stay with us but ... my Nana and Granda are staying with us till the end of the War.'

'I don't want to leave this place. I mean ... all this is mine now. And I'd rather be with you than strangers.' He held out his hand. Chas felt very strange. He had prickles up and down his spine. He felt bigger and stronger than ever before, and yet more frightened at the same time. He clasped the proffered hand in both of his.

'We'll have a meeting. We'll see you through.'

Nicky showed the pale ghost of a smile. 'I know where there's a lot of food ... that Petty Officer that got killed was in the Black Market. The old stables are full of stuff.'

'O.K. Let's get it before somebody else does. It'll mean enlarging the Fortress, though.'

More work for funny old John.

Everyone listened as Nicky told his story. Audrey sat picking at the scabs on her knees. Cem didn't laugh for once.

When Nicky had finished, they looked at each other in a long silence.

'We must tell some grown-up,' said Carrot-juice. 'They all think he's dead. It'll be in the records at the Town Hall and things. People will be worrying.'

'Who?' asked Clogger. 'Who is there who cares?' There was silence. Carrot-juice set his face stubbornly.

'Grown-ups know what's best!'

'They dae what's best for grown-ups,' said Clogger. 'They'll tidy him awa' into a Home and forget him, like they did wi' me when Ma died. They gie ye porridge wi'out sugar and belt ye if ye leave your shoes lying aboot.'

92

'He could stay with one of us,' said Audrey.

'Would *your* ma hae him?'

Audrey hung her head. She knew what her mother would say. They all knew what their mothers would say.

'But where can he live?'

'He could manage here,' said Clogger. 'We've got grub for a year. I've known folks put up wi' worse in Glasgow.'

'Suppose he gets ill?'

'Tek him tey the doctor. Plenty kids gan on their own, noo.'

'But won't he get lonely?'

Then quite an awful thing happened: Nicky began to cry and he couldn't stop. It was nothing like the way kids cry when they fall and hurt themselves. Words came bubbling out of his mouth about his father and his mother and that man and hate and death. Everyone was rooted to the spot. Then all the boys looked at Audrey.

She took a timid step forward and stroked his hair gingerly. It didn't make him any worse. She began to say his name gently, over and over.

'Everyone do it!' So they knelt and stroked his hair, his back, his arms, his knees.

'Nicky ... Nicky ... Nicky.'

In the end he stopped crying, sniffed and said, 'M'all right now. Sorry.' Audrey gave him her hanky and he wiped his face.

'He'd better no live here alone,' said Clogger. 'Ah'll come and live wi' him.'

'But what'll your auntie say?'

'Ah'll mek her think Ah've gone home tey Glasgow.'

'But she'll be worried sick.'

'Not her. She's not really ma auntie – just ma ma's cousin. She wasn't sae keen tey have me in the first place, and we're sleeping three in a bed. She'll miss the money ma dad sends, that's all.'

'But doesn't she ... love you?' Chas blushed as he said it.

'Love me? You kids don't know you're born. All she and ma uncle love is their beer and fags. Ah've thought of running away many a time ...' Everyone stared at him aghast, so that even Clogger became uncomfortable. 'Ah'll be away, then. Ah'll have to hurry if Ah'm tey get back afore dark.'

'Before you go ...' said Chas.

'Aye?'

'Everyone swear ... on the gun.' So they brought the gun out of its wrapping, and laid Granda's Union Jack on it, and everyone put their hands on the gun and swore to look after Nicky. In the swearing, Fortress Caparetto became more than a game; it became a nation. And the Germans ceased to be the only enemies. All the adults were a kind of enemy now, except John.

Clogger returned long after nightfall, his old bike laden with gear. He came by the back way – the loose boards in the fence.

'Easy! Ah left a note for ma auntie whilst they were snoozin' off their dinner. Ah biked tey Otterburn an' posted a postcard there. They'll think Ah'm away ower the Scottish border by noo.'

Nicky really smiled.

'I'm glad you're back. I'll get your supper.'

The police sergeant went round the homes of all Clogger's mates and questioned them. But it was easy to be stony-faced and lie, when you pretended you were a French Resistance fighter, and he was a Gestapo swine.

At each house the sergeant sensed something in the boy he talked to: not guilt, but hostility and cunning.

At McGill's, the last house, he turned to Chas's father on the doorstep.

'This war's doing bad things to kids. They're running wild. You don't know where you are with them any more. These are decent kids from decent homes; but they go on more like slum kids with a dad in the nick. You know, against the police on principle.'

'Mevve that says more about the police than the kids.' Mr McGill spat on the doorstep, and turned away to shut the door in the sergeant's face.

'Look,' said the sergeant desperately, jamming his foot in the door, 'they're up to something...'

'Take your foot out of my house,' said Mr McGill dangerously.

The sergeant left. But Mr McGill *was* worried about Chas for all his fighting words. He beckoned Chas to come into the cold front room, with its big chiming clock. Chas trembled; he knew what was coming.

He couldn't even pretend his father was some kind of Gestapo swine, like the police sergeant, or the Head flexing his cane. His father understood how kids really felt about things; more than most. Ever since he was little, Dad had meant safety: large, solid, bristly-faced, smelling of tobacco. His thumb always grew in three segments, where he had hit it with a hammer while he was an apprentice.

But could any grown-up keep you safe now? They couldn't stop the German bombers. They hadn't saved Poland, or Norway or France. Or the battleship the German submarine torpedoed in Scapa Flow itself.

Their own air-raid shelter at home – it wasn't as safe as the Fortress. It was only covered with a foot of soil. Couldn't Dad have done better than that?

He looked at his father, and saw a weary, helpless middle-aged man. Dad wasn't any kind of God any more. Chas screwed himself up to lie.

And for some reason Dad made it easy; maybe because

he was just so tired. He never looked at Chas. He took the big family Bible off the sideboard and made Chas swear on it that he knew nothing about machine-guns or Clogger. And Dad didn't even believe in God.

Chas swore with his eyes on the Bible. He could never have done it looking at his dad.

It all worked like a charm. With John's help they dug up the second Anderson shelter – the small one intended for the Nichol family. They made it entirely underground; buried deep, it could only be reached by a tunnel from the big one. They filled it with food and useful things from the bombed house – enamel jugs and bowls and mirrors.

Nothing from the bomb-damage was wasted. Another foot of rubble was piled over the Fortress. The gun-emplacement was roofed in with old doors and soil. Only the three loop-holes for the gun showed from the outside, and that was the way you got in.

They worked on the garden, too, directing the waters of the tiny stream with dams, so that the whole area became an ankle-deep swamp through which no one could pass.

At the other side, they fixed a whole section of fence so it would fall outward when someone pulled a rope from inside the Fortress. That gave what Lieutenant Andrew Morgan had called a good field of fire.

Audrey uprooted plants and privet-bushes and planted them on top for camouflage.

All was ready, just in time.

But not all the Fortress's defences were made by hands; some were made with mouths.

It was queer how rumours got around about the Nichol house. It became even more notorious in death than in life. Some people said there was another bomb there, unexploded, never found. Others reckoned there were ghosts; ghostly scrawlings of sailor obscenities on walls; laughter in a lighted bedroom which no longer had a floor.

Perhaps it was the fact that it looked so undamaged, though so many had died there. People pointed out its gables above the trees to visiting strangers. But no one went there, except the children.

EIGHT

Frost lay on the branches, and froze Clogger's breath on the eyepiece of the telescope. He wiped it angrily with his glove. But it was impossible to be really unhappy on such an evening. The sky was a dimming blue from horizon to horizon. The January evenings were beginning to draw out. Clogger consulted the old watch-and-chain that the lookouts always carried in their top pockets. Five o'clock. Fifteen minutes more in the Crow's Nest. He scanned the horizon with the telescope again. He was shivering so much that the horizon jumped round like a kangaroo.

Then he sucked in his breath. There was a dot, low over the waves. He lost it, and couldn't find it again. A stream of frightful Glaswegian words escaped his lips. When he finally spotted it again, it was nearer. He could see it had two engines.

'Captain, sir?' Chas's head emerged from a loophole.

'Plane, sir. Twin-engined, flying low.'

'Scarper!' shouted Chas. 'Gun out!' They whipped the silver fabric off the gun, and pushed the muzzle past Clogger as he scrambled in.

'Ey, watch it. I don't want a hole where ma dinner is!'

Chas gripped the gun and peered down the gunsight.

'Lower the fence!' Cem undid the knotted rope and the section of fence fell away, revealing the view over the bay. There was nothing in sight.

'Oh, *no*! *Another* false alarm! Clogger, you been at your uncle's whisky again?'

'There *was* something. Ah tell ye. It's too far off to see wi'out the telescope yet. Wait.'

And soon, there it was: a British plane, a Blenheim? Chas's eyes watered with the strain of looking. It was very low for a British plane. But perhaps it was damaged?

No. The propellers had that same queer windmill look. It was gliding in, with its engines shut off. It was black. It was *him*. And, as before, it would pass right overhead.

He lined up the sights on it. It grew bigger and bigger. Wait, wait. Finger on the curving trigger.

'Go *on*!' said Clem, and nudged him.

There was a flash and a roar. Something hit Chas in the chest, much harder than Boddser Brown's fist. He fell over backwards, pulling the gun with him. He lay on the ground with the thing still punching away at his chest. Wood splinters and soil rained down. He stared aghast at a gaping hole in the roof; through which he saw the German plane, crosses and all, pass as in a dream. It looked completely unharmed.

The tremendous banging of the gun ceased. Cem stared at the enormous hole in the roof.

'Cor blimey.'

The stream of bullets from the machine-gun missed the German fighter by miles. But it startled the pilot so much he put the plane into a near-vertical climb and nearly stalled. While he was battling to regain control, he was spotted by a lone pom-pom gunner on the Bank Top, who had been seeing to his gunsight. Long lines of red stitching followed the fighter up the sky.

More pom-poms opened up. One blew off the fighter's wing-tip and that seemed to drive the pilot mad. Far from trying to escape, he started a personal vendetta against the pom-poms. Once he came so low, he curved round the lighthouse on the Bank Top at zero feet, causing a fat woman with a pram to faint at the entrance to Chapel Street.

The end to such mad behaviour was inevitable. Three

99

Spitfires from Acklington got between him and the sea. But the pilot seemed beyond caring. He headed straight for the Spitfires, guns blazing. They were still blazing when he blew up over the harbour mouth. You could hear people cheering on both sides of the river.

What with the explosion and the cheering, nobody had noticed a small dark mass that had detached itself from the Messerschmidt at the last possible moment. It fell nearly to the ground before a parachute opened, and it still hit the ground rather hard.

Sergeant Rudi Gerlath, of the victorious Luftwaffe tried to stand up, but his ankle was agony. So he crawled instead, gathering the tell-tale folds of parachute as he went, into a clumsy bundle. He was in some sort of garden. Apart from the forest of brussels sprouts around him, the only cover was some little wooden sheds.

He crawled to the first shed, and opened the door, only to be greeted by a frantic clucking and fluttering. Hens! And where there were hens, people came to feed them. No go. He shut the door and crawled on. The next hut contained one big fat rabbit, who regarded Rudi thoughtfully while chewing his way up a long dandelion leaf.

'Rabbit, I envy you,' said Rudi. 'Rabbits live longer than rear gunners.'

The next hut was empty, except for spades and sacks. Rudi climbed in painfully, pulling the muddy parachute after him. He looked at his ankle. It wasn't broken or even bleeding. Just sprained so he couldn't walk.

Might as well surrender, he thought. Might be a hot meal before interrogation. I'd reveal all the secrets of the Third Reich for a glass of schnapps and a lump of sausage.

He opened the hut door and shouted loudly. Nobody came. Eventually he got tired of shouting and fell asleep.

The glare of the exploding plane, right overhead, did queer things to Chas's eyes. Everything he looked at had a glowing blue hole in it, the shape and size of the explosion. He wondered whether he would go permanently blind. It would be a tragic loss to the world. He heard a BBC announcer's voice in his head say, *He could have been the finest brain-surgeon England has ever seen. Even blind he is a superb concert pianist ... but how sad he should never see the blue sky again ...*

He went on walking round in circles and peering at things. The hole in his eyes seemed to be fading. He suddenly felt hungry and wondered what was for tea.

Cem was capering like a dervish on top of the Fortress, pulling up Audrey's camouflage-bushes and whirling them round his head.

'We got him, we got him!'

'You and how many Spitfires,' said Audrey acidly. 'You've certainly blown a fine hole in our roof with that thing.'

'Stop squabbling you two,' announced Chas with tears in his eyes. 'A brave man has died. He died facing his foes. What more can any man hope for?' He felt all grand and squashy inside, like when they played *Land of Hope and Glory* at school.

But the next second he felt cross because the Messerschmidt had blown up above the waters of the harbour, and there wouldn't be any souvenirs to pick up.

'What about that hole in the roof?' asked Audrey again. 'And next time you might kill somebody with that nasty great gun.'

'That's what it's for – that's what I was trying to do, so! Anyway, what do stupid girls know about it? Besides he –' he pointed to Cem – 'that stupid laughing fool jogged my arm.'

101

'Weren't that,' said Cem. 'You couldn't hold the gun steady. You're puny, that's your trouble.'

'Nobody could have held it,' said Chas. 'It kicks like a mule. You haven't even tried firing it.'

'Garn, Errol Flynn did it in that film. He charged the Jerries firing from the hip and won the VC.'

'You're wrong. Only British can get the VC,' shouted Audrey.

'Girls!' they all shouted together. 'What do *girls* know about it?' And then they went back to squabbling.

'You can't believe what's on *films*. Wasn't a real machine-gun.'

'Was. It was flashing.'

'Wasn't.'

'Was.'

'Wasn't.'

'What about that hole in the roof? *And* I'm not going back into the camp to make tea until you put that nasty great thing away.'

'SHURRUP.'

'Och, we'd better do as she says, or we'll no get a cup o' tea. And ye'd better find some way of holding that gun down. It nearly shot ma head off.'

'My dad could make a stand to hold it.'

'Ah dare say he could. But how ye going to ask him? Ye can hardly say "Da make us a stand for me real loaded machine-gun".'

Chas looked thoughful.

'I can get him to make me one. But I'll have to borrow the telescope for a few days.'

'Why not? There's nowt left to watch out for now, any way.'

Rudi wakened, stiff and cold. No matter how carefully

he arranged them, the sacks fell off him during the night. His ankle was up like a pudding; he wouldn't be able to walk for a week.

He opened the hut door and looked out. The sky was grey. His watch had stopped and there was no way of telling the time. He was terribly hungry. Even the frosted brussels sprouts began to seem appetising. He spent an hour crawling over and gathering some. He had to suck the frost out of them before he could chew them. They were as hard as bullets.

He wished he could surrender. But no one came. He fell asleep.

When he awakened again, the sky was still grey. He was beginning to lose feeling in his legs. When he finally got the circulation back, the pins and needles were awful.

He decided to crawl in and surrender. It seemed a hundred miles to the edge of the allotments. When he got to the fence and looked through a gap, there was only a cinder track, a disused gas-lamp and the high brick wall of some factory. It was getting dark and starting to snow, so he had to crawl all the way back. He became so confused he couldn't find his hut at first. He slept again.

It was the rabbits who saved him that week. Most of the huts contained a few. In their hutches he found food; crusts of toast, baked potato-peelings, bran-mash, drinkable water. In the beginning the beasts bolted when he opened their hutch-doors to steal their dinner; bundles of warm, panicky fur hurled themselves from one side to the other, pressing their panting sides into patterns against the hutch-wire. He contemplated killing one for the meat, but he wasn't desperate enough yet.

After five days the rabbits got used to him, and eyed him placidly. He spent hours in their company, giving them pet names – Birgit, Franz, Heinz. He talked to them, and they seemed to listen, drooping first one ear and then the other.

When were they fed? Why did he never see the owners? He couldn't tell. He contemplated sleeping with them, waiting to be captured. But he had an aversion to being taken in his sleep. Besides, a distrust of all humans was setting in. Not the fear of a prisoner-of-war for his enemies, but the distrust of a wild animal, daily growing wilder.

He only saw one other human being in all his time on the allotment – an old man picking brussels sprouts. It took Rudi a long time to pluck up courage to shout and wave. The old man gave one panicky look and ran. Rudi expected him back with soldiers, but he didn't come. Perhaps the old man had been a thief and hadn't realised Rudi was a German.

Chas knew very well how to approach his dad. He carried the telescope home and dumped it in front of him.

'Where'd you get that?'

'Cem Jones wants a swop. It was his grandad's. He wants my train set. Is it worth it?' Mr McGill reached for the telescope, turning it over in his clever mechanic's hands, feeling the solid craftsmanship.

'Cem Jones is a fool. This is worth a lot more than your trainset. Does his dad know he's swapping it?'

'Yeah, he was there. He said this was mucky old rubbish and not worth a good train set. He said *I* was a fool.' Mr McGill bridled. He didn't like Mr Jones; there was a long-standing row between the families.

'That man knows nowt but tombstones. A bairn could see this is a good piece of stuff.' Already he was taking the telescope to pieces. 'Needs a bit of seeing to, though. Go and fetch me tools and the Brasso.'

It was a peaceful evening, like one before the War.

Granda was better, and had gone off to the pub to have a crack with his mates. Nana was skinning a rabbit in the kitchen, her brawny red arms snowed with tufts of fur. Mrs McGill put some potatoes to bake next the fire, in their jackets. Mr McGill worked on the telescope, laying out parts in careful order on a sheet of newspaper. How would he ever get them together again? But he did, gleaming and shining; pointing out things of interest to Chas as he did so.

'Can I swop then?'

'Aye; you're growing up, and a railway's a bairn's thing. Better not show the telescope to Mr Jones now, though, or he'll change his mind. Old rubbish, indeed. The man's an idiot.'

Now was the moment. Chas took a deep breath.

'Only trouble is, Dad, it's so heavy. I can't hold it steady.' Mr McGill looked up at him with a slow grin.

'I knew there'd be a catch. Want me to make you a tripod for it?'

'Yeah!' In his moment of triumph, Chas felt a rat. It was a much worse pain than parting with his beloved railway.

Mr McGill was good at his work. He liked a technical problem, and he had time to solve it. The gasworks for once did not break down. The tripod was finished in a week.

Mr McGill made things to last, in quarter-inch steel and inch gas-pipe, solidly welded together, and given a black finish to proof it against rust. The tripod held the round body of the telescope just fine. It would hold the round body of the machine-gun equally well, and if the legs were bedded in concrete ...

NINE

'Got a funny case here, Sarge,' said Fatty Hardy. The sergeant groaned. More than bombers or the coming Invasion, he dreaded Fatty Hardy's funny cases. Pinched sandbags, missing machine-guns, haunted houses ... The constable was a lunatic.

'What is it *this* time?'

'It's a woman with a funny story.'

'Let her in to tell it then. I haven't had a laugh in weeks.'

'I didn't mean a *joke,* Sarge.' Hardy looked baffled.

'Oh, send her in and *go.*'

The woman perched herself on the edge of a chair like a bird, clasped her hands and closed her eyes.

'Let us pray,' said the sergeant, before he could stop himself. It was the tiredness that did it.

'Let us pray indeed, young man. For these are the Latter Days when the Foul Beast shall be loosed from the Pit. Book of Revelation, chapter thirteen, verse eleven.'

Oh Lord, thought the sergeant, she's one of those.

'What is more, the servants of the Foul Beast have been machine-gunning my mother.'

'Your what?' gasped the sergeant, nearly falling out of his chair.

'Three days ago, as I live and breathe, I'd just taken Mother her cup of tea and was reading to her from the Good Book when something came through our roof and smashed the *God is Love* that hangs over her bed.'

'What sort of something?' asked the sergeant cautiously. The woman dug in her purse and dropped a flattened bullet into his hand. The sergeant could see it wasn't British.

'What happened then?'

'I ran to the window and saw their Fearsome Machine fleeing God's Wrath, going straight up into the Heavens.'

A strange choice of direction, thought the sergeant, but caught his tongue in time.

'German?'

'It bore the Crooked Cross.' The sergeant tossed the bullet thoughtfully up and down. It had been that German fighter that exploded all right; the one everybody called the Tea-time Sneaker.

'Where do you live?'

'Simpson Street – across the river. Are you the War Damage?'

'Am I *what*?'

'The War Damage. Mrs Spink said if I reported it to the War Damage, they'd come and mend the hole in our roof, and give us a new *God is Love*.'

'Madam, I am *not* the War Damage. But leave your address and I will send round the man who is.' The woman sniffed and left.

The sergeant sat on. It didn't make sense. The Tea-time Sneaker had been a reconnaissance plane, relying on stealth. Why should it open fire on a street miles from any military target?

Nervous rear-gunner? But Simpson Street lay at right-angles to the Sneaker's flight-path. Even a nervous rear-gunner would not turn his gun through ninety degrees of slipstream before going trigger-happy.

Were they all mad in that plane? It had climbed vertically immediately afterwards, which was a mad enough thing to do. Or had something upset a normally steady crew?

Something like being fired on from the ground? By a machine-gun whose bullets missed and landed among houses across the river? But they were *German* bullets . . .

The sergeant banged his fist on the desk and swore. That missing machine-gun. What a fool he'd been.

The sergeant surveyed *God is Love* and its line of bullet holes. The text was not alone on the bedroom walls at Simpson Street. *God Bless this house* with a border of blue kittens and pansies hung above the empty fireplace. *Thou God seest Me* stitched round a large and malevolent eye, hung over the door.

Not only God's eye surveyed the sergeant; the bright beady eyes of the old lady in the bed followed him everywhere.

"Aven't gorra fag, 'ave ya? I'm right gasping. She won't let me 'ave them, yer know. Says they're ungodly. Her and her God. She's potty, yer know. It's a case when a pore old body can't 'ave 'er death-bed comforts.'

The sergeant offered a bent Woodbine and lit it. She sucked in smoke, her face wreathed in beatific smiles. Like a baby having its bottle.

'That's the first this week. Mrs Davies slips me one when she calls, but she's laid up with her sciatica.'

'Where d'you put the ash?' asked the sergeant nervously. The old lady pointed to the rose-wreathed chamber-pot under her bed.

'Last time the doctor came to test me water 'e nearly 'ad a fit.'

'Excuse *me*,' said the sergeant. He must get on with his job. He tied a piece of string with a weight on the end to the bullet holes in the ceiling. Then he put his head against the shattered *God is Love* and looked beyond the string, through the window. He was now looking down the path the bullets had come . . . they had come from a clump of trees across the river, with a chimney-pot sticking up through them . . .

'Help!' gasped the old lady, breaking into a paroxysm

of coughing. The sergeant thought she was starting a fit, her eyes were swivelling wildly. But he finally realised she wanted him to take the cigarette.

He had just taken it when the daughter burst in. The old lady must have hearing like radar!

'Smoking!' said the daughter triumphantly. Her eyes alighted on the Woodbine in the sergeant's hand. 'This whole rooms stinks like the Foul Pit.'

'I told 'im you wouldn't have smoking, Ada,' said the old woman, 'but he wouldn't heed. He took advantage of me lying here 'elpless.'

'So *you* say. I'll think my own thoughts about what happens to those who abuse God's Truth, on Judgement Day. Meanwhile, Sergeant, I'll ask you to leave. You're only here on sufferance. You're not even War Damage.'

'Madam, I have my job to do.'

'What's that? And what's this rubbish?' She pulled at the string that dangled from the ceiling. It came loose, pulling half the ceiling with it.

'Look at all me plaster. On me best carpet. Get out, or I'll set the police on you.'

'Madam, I *am* the police.'

'Have you got a search warrant?' she screamed. The sergeant decided it was time to Flee the Foul Tempter.

All the way back over the river on the ferry, he tried to work out which was the little clump of trees on the north bank he had seen beyond the string. But there were so many clumps. It would be a long job finding it.

At last came the morning when Rudi found he could walk. But walk where? To a policeman, a prison camp? It was tempting. Warm blankets, a bath, hot soup and bread, comrades who spoke German. But the problem was getting safe to the prison camp.

He knew how much Garmouth had been bombed. Night after night he had lain under a thin wooden roof while bombs rained down; while searchlights revolved like the spokes of giant wheels; while fires burned and the bells of fire-engines clanged through the streets.

People who had been bombed hated enemy fliers. Rudi had seen the capture of a British flier in Berlin, the first night it had been bombed. The man stumbled along between two Wehrmacht, who used their fixed bayonets to keep the German civilians back; civilians who threw stones and dog-dirt at the airman and his captors alike. One woman had leapt in screaming and clawed the flier's face. That was when the officer had ordered his soldiers to fire their rifles in the air. But suppose the soldiers hadn't been there? There were stories of airmen hanged from lamp-posts, run through with pitchforks.

Rudi opened the holster on his belt. Alone of his possessions, the Luger pistol was clean. That would deal with those who brought ropes and pitchforks.

Then there was the pain of being a prisoner. All his life Rudi had hated being fastened in. Once he had run away from the *oberschule* because the master had locked him in a cupboard. All his boyhood he had roamed the streets, until his mother accused him of turning into a criminal. But he was never a criminal; he just had to be free.

But where could he go to stay free? He must stick to wasteland, where no English went; old dumps and bombed houses. And he would walk to the sea, which the British called the North Sea and the Germans the German Ocean. There might be a boat he could steal, or a Swedish cargo-ship to stow away on. It was a forlorn hope, but before he was captured or killed he would look once more on the sea.

He closed his holster; fastened one large sack round his

middle with a lump of rope, and draped another, marked *Al Cattle Cake* over his flying helmet. He must keep on his flying helmet, or else he could be shot as a spy. He thought with his new beard and mud-encrusted trousers he might pass as a tramp.

He said good-bye to the rabbits, and stuffed his pockets with frozen brussels sprouts. Then he set off, beginning to sing to himself in that peculiar monotone he had heard tramps use in his childhood. It was a bitterly cold day; not many people were about. But as he was cutting down a back lane, a woman came out to her dustbin with a dish of scraps; a stout body in a flowered apron and checked carpet-slippers. She stared at the approaching shambling figure. Rudi hummed *Ich hatt' einen kameraden* in a high-pitched whine. He looked at the scraps hungrily; cabbage and lumps of pie-crust.

The hand that was scraping them into the bin with a knife paused. Rudi halted and looked up, making his eyes wide so the white showed all round.

'Where *you* from?' asked the woman. Rudi understood her; he had done English at *oberschule*. But he daren't reply, for his accent was strong. Instead he mouthed gibberish, and pointed first to the plate, and then at his mouth. The woman's face melted from doubt to kindliness. She offered the plate timidly. Rudi clawed up the scraps and thrust them into his mouth. Even in his fear they tasted marvellous.

'Wait!' said the woman, holding up her hand. She vanished back into her yard. Rudi wondered whether to run, but he couldn't. His ankle was too painful and the back lane was too long. He waited what seemed a lifetime, until the woman reappeared with half a loaf and a large wizened apple. Now there was a man behind her, her husband doubtless. He had a bald head, a thrusting chin, a collarless shirt and red braces, into which he stuck his thumbs aggressively.

111

'What you hanging round here for, pestering women?'

'Meerp, meerp, ugama,' said Rudi, earnestly.

'Hush, Jack,' said the woman, 'can't you see he's a dumbie?'

'Riff-raff,' said her husband. 'I'd shoot the likes of those. No use to the War Effort at all.'

'How much use are you, always on the Sick with your back?' asked the woman, a spark kindling in her eye. 'Leave the poor thing alone. He's not doing you any harm.' She thrust loaf and apple into Rudi's hands. 'Here yar, love, and the best of luck.'

'Ug, ug, meerp,' said Rudi, and shambled away. He could hear the man and woman start to quarrel as they entered the house.

Rudi wandered on till he found a bombed house in a huge wooded garden. The gates were wired together, but he got over them somehow. The house was abandoned. But it had water trickling from a burst pipe in what had been the kitchen; and one room still had a roof, and glass in the windows. There were old pink mattresses thrown about, and torn curtains for bedding. Even plenty of broken wood for a fire, if he had only had matches. Why, he could live here for weeks.

He settled down and ate the apple, and half of the bread. He made himself leave the rest till later. He'd been luckier than he deserved; the tramp disguise was working. It would not have worked in Germany. There were no tramps there now. Hitler had put them into hospitals and they were never seen again.

He started. Footsteps sounded on the gravel drive. He peeped round the filthy curtain. A man in a blue uniform was staring at the house. Gestapo? Did the British have Gestapo? He wore no gun, carried no truncheon, but wore a tall pointed hat. *Polizei*! The man limped and looked very tired. Even in his own present state, Rudi felt sorry for him. It would be a pity to shoot him.

Was this the moment to surrender? It would be so easy, that walk to the *polizei* barracks. What could seem more harmless to hostile civilians than a *polizei* walking with an old tramp? And once in a cell, he would be safe from ropes and pitchforks.

But Rudi was a gambler at heart: on horses, at cards, even on racing two cockroaches. And at the moment his luck was holding.

He heard the sergeant enter the house; heard his heavy boots echoing from room to room, coming nearer. All Rudi could do was get behind the door, Luger in one hand, loaf of bread in the other.

The door opened; the sergeant's helmeted head appeared. It seemed to Rudi he was looking for something on the floor, not for a person. Rudi held his breath, finger on trigger.

The door closed. Rudi waited till the footsteps receded, and then took several great panting breaths. The sergeant left the house, and went round the back. Rudi crept from room to room, watching him. The back garden was wild and huge, with old statues and urns overthrown by the bomb's blast. The sergeant began to walk among them, down towards the back fence where a mound of tumbled rubble lay under the trees.

The sergeant paused, and then began to pick his way gingerly. Suddenly, his shiny boot vanished up to the ankle.

'Damn and Hell!' The sergeant slipped and nearly fell, hanging on to a sundial for support. His boots were covered in thick yellow mud. He shrugged, and turned back towards the house, rubbing his boots on the long grass as he came. He passed, and his footsteps faded.

Immediately, Rudi felt the call of nature. Quick; the last thing he wanted was wet trousers. But not in the house.

113

He might be there for days, and he couldn't stand the smell of a place where someone had urinated.

He'd go down the garden, under the trees. He grinned; the mud wouldn't put *him* off; his flying boots couldn't get any muddier. With difficulty, he reached the trees. He looked back, to make sure nobody was watching. Funny, that house looked familiar ... where had he seen it before? He couldn't have seen it before. He'd been once on holiday in England before the War, but that was Brighton, hundreds of miles south. You're getting delirious, *kamerad*, he thought to himself.

After he had been among the trees, he felt much better, and stared about. There was a little doorway in that mound of rubble, not much bigger than a rabbit hole; in fact there were three doorways, all in a row. What was it, a bomb-shelter? A coal cellar? Rudi couldn't resist his curiosity; he had a feeling he was being foolish, but he *had* to know what was inside. Down the hole he went.

He straightened up, and looked straight down the barrel of a machine-gun. By the light of a candle, he could see four helmeted figures crouching over the gun.

His luck had ended with a vengeance. He put up his hands, as high in the air as he could push them. As he did so, the sacks fell from his waist and head.

TEN

CLOGGER had done a wonderful job with the concrete floor. He'd even got the holes in the right place, so that the tripod fitted in neatly. They brought out the gun and screwed it into the tripod. It swung easily and precisely, covering land and sky. It would certainly never jump about again, a menace to life and limb. Now it would fire where it was pointed.

'Might as well change the magazines,' said Cem. After a lot of fiddling, the empty magazine was removed.

'I'll just test the gun while it's empty,' said Chas. He pulled the trigger and there was a satisfying sharp click. But when Cem insisted on trying it, there was no click; the trigger felt slack, dead.

'Try pulling all the levers,' suggested Cem. They pushed and pulled everything for ten minutes, but the trigger remained dead. Even (amidst Audrey's protests) putting a full magazine on made no difference.

'You've bloody broken it,' said Chas in disgust

'It was broken 'fore I touched it,' said Cem. 'Was you.'

'Wasn't, so.'

'Was, so.'

'Och, gie us a go at sorting it then,' said Clogger. 'Ma dad could aye mend watches.'

What else was there to do? What good is a gun that won't fire?

'All right, but be careful.'

They watched hopefully. His fingers seemed to sure and clever. He loosened one nut, then another. Then there was a *ping*, and a shower of shiny pieces fell all over the new concrete floor.

'Crikey!'

'Don't worry; Ah can mend it.'

'You and whose army?'

Clogger got on his hands and knees and began frantically picking up the pieces. 'Gie out o' ma light,' he grunted angrily.

But somebody was scrambling down the loophole to get in. Somebody ... they froze with horror. The somebody was big, an adult. And it wasn't John. It was a stranger; an adult stranger.

Chas felt his stomach pull together in a tight knot, the way a spider does when you touch it.

This wasn't real; this was a nightmare. The dead German air-gunner had come back for his gun, helmet and all! It was like his Granda's nightmare, when the Austrian soldier came back for his hat-badge! Chas grabbed the machine-gun; even a dead air-gunner wasn't going to take his treasure.

But the German had his hands up!

'Quick, it's a Jerry. Get his gun.' The phrase sprang to his lips from so many war-films.

Clogger reacted, too, like someone in the movies, getting behind the German, patting around his waist for a weapon. He flipped open the holster, pulled out the Luger, and backed away to the wall of the shelter.

'*Dumkopf*!' said Rudi to himself bitterly. These were children, playing at soldiers. But the gun was real; it was the kind he used himself. He stared around, as his eyes got used to the candle-light; at the neatly-piled sandbags. *Were* these children or soldiers? Was the British Army as short of men, after Dunkirk, as the Fuehrer had said? Or was every Britisher armed, even children? Was England one vast armed camp, just waiting to massacre any poor Ger-

116

man who landed? Were these the awful English, who would fight on the beaches, as Churchill said? It was very confusing.

For a long time they all stared at each other, then Rudi said. 'Please, hands down? Mein arms tired are.'

'*Hande hoch!*' screamed Clogger, pulling back the round handle on top of the Luger. That, too, was what they did in the movies.

Steady, thought Rudi. I must be calm or I'll get my head blown off. He said carefully and slowly, 'Please may I down sit? I tired am.'

'Let him, Clogger. It's safer.' Clogger nodded, and gestured down at the concrete floor with the pistol-barrel. Rudi sat down very slowly, and put his hands on the back of his neck. Only his eyes moved, here and there. Who were these kids? The British version of the Hitler Youth? Another was pointing a long black air-rifle at him.

He glanced at the machine-gun. It was on a good solid mounting, but it was stripped down. It couldn't have been fired anyway. He'd been fooled. Now they were holding him prisoner with his own *verdammt* pistol, which was dangerously cocked. They were passing it gingerly from one to the other. Oh, Rudi, Rudi, he thought, lifting his eyes to the ceiling, if only your mother could see you now! Perhaps they would fetch soldiers soon, and the soldiers would take him away to a nice safe prison-camp.

'What we going to *do*?' screamed Cem. 'He's a *Nazi*!'

'He's no sae like a proper Nazi,' said Clogger dubiously. And indeed the tattered wretch before them was not much like those black shiny-booted stormtroopers who goosestepped nightly through their dreams.

'He ain't got no swastikas!'

'He's not a blond beast!'

117

'He looks hungry,' said Audrey. 'Can I give him a mug of tea?'

'S'pose so,' said Chas, grudgingly. The German slowly removed his flying-helmet, and sucked at the tea noisily. His hair was long, black and greasy, and going a bit grey at the sides, like Mr McGill's. He really looked like somebody's dad; a bit fed-up and tired.

'What *are* we going to do with him?'

'Take him to the Warden's Post.'

'What, with a loaded Luger stuck in his back? That'll cause a few questions. Besides, he'd tell them about us.'

'But he can't speak English.'

'He can, a bit. Besides, they'll interrogate him in German. Errol Flynn did, in that film. Then he'll split about the Fortress and the machine-gun, and then we've had it.'

'But they're only supposed to give their name, rank and number. That's in the Geneva Convention.'

'The what?'

'The Geneva Convention.'

'What do you know about the Geneva Convention?'

'My dad told me.'

'Och, tripe.'

'Besides, that only means he musn't tell the interrogators anything about *Germany* – it doesn't mean he won't split on us.'

Rudi watched their worried faces woozily. It was warm in here, with the smell of paraffin. He hadn't been warm for a week. He was so tired ... the place was going dark ...

'Hey, he's falling to sleep!'

'Better get him inside. Hey, raus, RAUS.' Rudi sat up with a bewildered jerk.

'Poor sod, he's knackered.' Clogger pointed towards the interior of the Anderson with his pistol-barrel. Rudi went like a sleep-walker. He had a blessed vision of a real bunk, a patchwork quilt, and then he knew no more. The children looked at his snoring shape.

'Blimey!'

ELEVEN

'IT's getting near the spring tides,' opined Mr McGill, looking up from the *Daily Express*. 'That's when They'll come, mark my words.'

'But it's not spring yet,' said Mrs McGill, 'it's only February.'

'I don't mean that kind of spring, woman. A spring tide's when the sea's higher than usual. It'll carry their flat-bottomed barges up over the beach defences.'

'What's flat-bottomed barges, Dad?'

Mr McGill laid down his paper. 'They're boats wi' flat bottoms, so they can get close ashore. Hitler's gathering all he can find in Holland and Belgium, and when he's ready, he'll tow them across full of soldiers, using tugs.'

'But they won't come this far north,' said Mrs McGill. 'They'll land on the Thames, or Liverpool or something.' Her grasp of geography was never great. Chas could never convince her that Edinburgh was not near London.

'Har,' said Mr McGill, 'mevve that's what Hitler and them *wants* us to think. They'll get aal our soldiers down south, and then they'll attack up here and cut the country in half.'

'Don't talk like that,' said his wife, 'or I shan't sleep safe in my bed.'

'That Hitler's liable to do anything,' said Nana. 'The crafty gyet. I reckon they don't watch the beach close enough. Hitler could nip ashore off one of them U-boats, and we'd never know he was here till he walked in the front door. And then I'd tell him a thing or two. I haven't forgotten Grandad's best top-coat, and them two china dogs they done for.

'Mother,' said Mr McGill patiently. 'Hitler wouldn't come on his own. He'd bring his whole army.'

'Aye, mevve. Ah only wish Granda was twenty years younger. He'd see him off.'

'Do you really think they'll come Dad?' said Chas, thinking of his own, personal, sleeping German.

'Well,' said Mr McGill in a businesslike way, 'Hitler can't afford to hang about for ever. We're getting stronger all the time; there's all those Canadian soldiers arriving on the newsreels, and we're churning out more and more Spitfires. By, I saw twenty-five all together, from the top of the gasholder yesterday, and a grand sight they looked.'

'Spitfires is too fond of flying about aal day like paper kites. What about at nights?' said Nana. 'They can't stop the Jarmans then.'

'*Mother*. The Spitfires cannot see them at nights.'

'Don't see why not. The Jarmans could see to bomb wor house. *And* split Granda's coat.'

'*They* can't see either. They were *aiming* for the ships in the river.'

'Why, they're blinder than a drunken sailor, then.'

'Mother, that's what I *said* . . .'

Were the Germans really coming, wondered Chas. If so, there'd be use for the machine-gun yet. But the gun was broken. Perhaps their prisoner could mend it? He wondered how Clogger and Nicky were getting on.

Rudi wakened as from a black pit. Someone had taken off his boots while he slept. He was deliciously warm, and there was a smell of frying.

'Here's ya breakfast.' He saw a determined face with freckles and a shock of ginger hair. The boy held a plate of fried bread and bacon in one hand, and the still-cocked pistol in the other.

121

Rudi took the plate, eyeing the gun nervously, and wolfed the food, and then felt again the call of nature. He made appropriate signals, embarrassed because one of the children was a girl.

They led him to a clump of bushes, well away from the camp, and watched him solemnly. He was glad to get back into his bunk. He was sweating, his legs were wobbly, and he had a racking cough. It was as if, having reached a place of safety, his body was exacting payment for what it had suffered. He fell asleep again, almost immediately.

'He's poorly.'

'Aye, he's got the bronchitis, Ah'm thinking.'

'Do you think he'll die?' asked Audrey. 'Should we fetch a doctor?'

'*No*,' they all chorused.

'We've got some cough mixture at home. I'll go and fetch it.'

Day and night ceased to exist for Rudi. Awake, he alternately shivered and sweated, scratching himself where his rucked-up trousers chafed his body. Asleep, he fended off endless Spitfires attacking from the blind-spot under the tail.

The only comfort was an endless succession of tea, cocoa, medicine and soup; and the worried face of the girl-child who spooned them into his mouth. Often, all the children would sit and watch him with that same worried look, until he was certain he was dying.

The children baffled him. They weren't ordinary children, like those he had played with at the *oberschule* before Hitler came. They were too solemn, too adult; except that even adults sometimes laughed.

But they were not solemn like those little pigs of Hitler

Youth, who swaggered everywhere in their swastika arm-bands, and would report you for getting drunk in uniform, or even walking down the street with a tunic button undone. If you criticized the bosses in Germany these days, the last place you did it was in a children's playground.

No, these children were strange in that they neither laughed or quarrelled. Oh, they argued, argued a lot. But they never fell out, or walked off in a huff. It was as if they depended on each other like ... the crew of a bomber. Sink or swim together.

Of course, they weren't always there. Only two never left. The one with red hair and freckles and a chin like a rock; nothing would ever shake that one. He was already a man. The other was nervous, with dark wistful eyes. He jumped at every noise. He was the weak point; the one who if Rudi was ever to escape, must be tricked, frightened, exploited.

But the dark one was a danger too. For the two boys guarded him alternately, sitting at the far end of the opposite bunk with the still-cocked Luger in their lap. Night and day, whenever he awakened, one or the other was there.

They held the pistol so differently. The red-head held it calmly, pointing out of the door, finger clear of the trigger; as quietly as a carpenter holds a hammer. But the dark one's fingers played constantly over the whole gun, worrying at it. Lugers had delicate triggers; even with the safety-catch on they could go off if you dropped them. In this metal box the bullet would ricochet round like a demented bee, till it found somebody's flesh.

That gun had to be uncocked for everyone's sake. The times the dark boy held it were no good; he was too jumpy. Rudi must wait till the red-head held it.

Stan Liddell had almost forgotten what it was like to be a schoolteacher. Every day as he walked past the school he looked up at the roof; every day the tail of the bomber mocked him. Workmen had tried stretching tarpaulins across the hole to make the roof watertight. But the wind first waved them like huge flags, and then blew them away. Rain dripped from floor to floor, ceaselessly.

The first week, Stan and the other teachers had salvaged books and globes and wall-charts. They organized classes for the school certificate forms in the games pavilions and groundsman's hut, and then they stuck. There were no church halls or cinemas or even churches available to teach in; they were being used as rest-centres and soup-kitchens for bombed-out families.

Life got more and more unreal for Stan. He would stop in the middle of teaching Chaucer to the Sixth and remember the Germans. For Stan had actually fought them, for three incredible months in 1918. Old Jerry wasn't a comic figure to Stan; Old Jerry was a grey flicker of distant men, who killed unerringly and were very hard to kill; Old Jerry was a tattered faceless corpse on the barbed wire, mud, stink and exploding chaos.

And Old Jerry was coming again. Already, in Stan's mind's eye, every Garmouth field was pitted with shell-holes, every neat terrace a row of eyeless windows, every winter tree not only leafless, but twigless and branchless.

It didn't bear thinking about, but Stan could not stop thinking. He watched every newsreel, read every newspaper that might tell him how Old Jerry had changed his tricks since 1918. For if Jerry crossed the sea, Garmouth Home Guard – eighty-four old men and boys – would be the first to greet him.

Stan lectured them, drilled them, taught them everything he knew. They were keen; but which were worse: the boys who treated it like a lark, or the old men who had fought on the Somme and the Marne, whose lungs wheezed every time they ran twenty yards.

They had rifles; rifles the Canadian Army had packed away in vaseline because they were out-of-date in 1912 ... rifles the Boer War had been fought with.

And a weapon against the invincible Panzers too! A lump of drainpipe with a foresight welded on by the local blacksmith; a pipe that fired rockets (when they didn't misfire and drop fizzing out of the front end, making everybody run for it). They had a target – an old car pulled along by a winch. It was plated up with corrugated iron, and given a wooden turret with a broomstick gun. They painted swastikas on it, and gave demonstrations to the public. Sometimes a rocket actually hit the crawling 'Jerry tank' and burst in a shower of blinding thermite, and set the wooden turret ablaze. Then the public would clap and cheer and slap each other on the back saying 'Jerry better not land here!' Didn't the fools know that German tanks had armour three inches thick? The Home Guard was a con, to keep the housewives feeling safe in their beds.

Yet it was to the Home Guard HQ that Stan walked every day. It was better than a wrecked school where plaster fell off the walls, and rusting desks oozed black water if you touched them with your finger.

It had Sandy.

That morning, Stan noticed, Sandy had been busy again. A bank of earth had been raked clean, and the legend 1ST COMPANY (GARMOUTH) HOME GUARD had been impressed with whitewashed stones.

'Morning, sar. Lovely morning. Think it's the day for Jerry?'

'Ah, um,' said Stan. It was raining.

'Two letters came for you, sar. Poster from Northern Command about disguised German paratroops.'

'Put it up,' said Stan. But he could see it was already up.

'And an offer of two shotguns from Farmer Moulton at Preston.'

'Sounds good!'

'They are, sar, they are. Came up nicely with a drop of oil.' Sandy indicated two new guns in the rifle-rack. 'No ammo, though. But I think I can win some from a mate at the War Ag. Told him we were terrible pestered with rabbits.'

'Sarnt-major!' said Stan, in the voice of dismayed approval that he knew Sandy expected.

'It's all for the War Effort, sar. Jerry could be here by lunch. Can't go over the top without ammo, sar. And I got a new copy of Fire Regulations from the Castle. They had a spare copy doing nothing, so I won it. Oh, and there's a civvy policeman to see you, sar.'

Stan tramped on upstairs in his thin shabby Home Guard uniform. He wore it all the time now. It made him feel better; more ready. The sergeant with a limp was sitting in in the company office.

'Not that machine-gun *again*?' said Stan irritably.

''Fraid so. Two more bits of evidence come up. Both trivial in themselves but ...'

'Go on!'

'First, I found an old complaint in the files from Mary Brownlee, mother of John Brownlee, a mental defective aged forty.'

'What's he been up to?'

'Getting himself dirty – plastered with clay and mud. His mother – she's a well-meaning body – always tries to keep him nice. Seems she hasn't been able to, recently. He comes home whacked, boots soaked.'

126

'What does *he* say about it?'

'Can't string two sensible words together. His mother's tried following him. When she does, he just wanders round in circles, keeping clean. But the moment her back's turned, he vanishes and comes back filthy.'

'No clue?'

'One. He's been seen in the company of guess who?'

'Charles McGill?'

'Right. They live in the same street. When he saw Mrs Brownlee watching, McGill sheered off, sharpish.'

'What's the other complaint?'

'Even more trivial. Man called Parton. Same pattern. Daughter stays out till all hours, comes home filthy.'

'Daughter's name Audrey? Red hair?'

'Yes. I've tried questioning her. Won't open her mouth, to me *or* her parents. They've tried hitting her, I'd guess, but it hasn't got them anywhere, and there's not much else they can do about it.'

'That'll be Audrey Parton of 3A at our school?'

'Yes. And McGill's in 3A, and Jones his little mate, and the Nichol boy who was supposed to be killed by that bomb, and the Duncan boy who ran off home to Glasgow. And the Brown boy who took that German flier's helmet is in 3B. It's all too much of a coincidence.'

'Supposed? But surely the Nichol boy *is* dead?'

'Well, if he is, he's the first case I've heard of, of death by bombing, that never left a trace. And young Duncan never showed up in any of his old Glasgow haunts – we checked.'

'So . . . ?'

'They've got that gun and they've built a hideout for it. Remember those sandbags that went missing? And Nichol and Duncan are living there, and the others are keeping them fed. I've checked all the families. The McGills keep on finding the odd pint of paraffin missing; the Partons are some candles short, and the Joneses a hurricane lamp. And there's been nicking from shops ... no proof, of course, they're too smart for that.'

Stan fought down a wave of exasperation with both kids and sergeant alike.

'Told your Inspector about this?'

The sergeant shrugged. 'I've tried. Trouble is Mr McGill keeps on complaining that we're harassing his son. I got a flea in my ear and instructions to lay off the case permanently.'

'And *had* you been harassing young McGill?'

'We've tried to follow him. No hope. He's on to us, and he's as fly as two monkeys. He's led us a dance for ten miles, and ended up throwing pebbles at tin cans in the river. You might as well try shadowing a seagull. He walks along the tops of walls, gets through holes in hedges a dog couldn't follow him into. Even my youngest constable can't keep up with him. And we haven't got the manpower ...'

The sergeant's voice went into a querulous wail, and it was all Stan could do to keep himself from laughing.

'How about following the others?'

'They're all the same, even the girl.'

'So why not leave them alone?'

'Another two feet and they'd have killed that old woman in Simpson Street. Can't *you* think of something, sir?'

'But they know me better than they know you ... oh ... let me think about it, sergeant.' The sergeant got up, relieved. He had dumped the problem on someone else's shoulders ... which was all he really wanted. Thanks very much, thought Stan.

He decided to go up to the observation platform on top of the mill. He always did that when he needed to think. The Home Guard shared the Polish binoculars and telephone with the Observer Corps. There was an observer on duty, purple with cold, his woolly scarf whipping in the drizzly breeze.

'All quiet?'

'All quiet. No Junkers 52s yet.' The man laughed abruptly, as if he'd made a poor joke, and as abruptly stopped.

'Junkers 52s?'

'Yeah, haven't you heard? Jerry always uses them to drop paratroopers ahead of an invasion. Did it in Norway, and in Holland. Usually they're disguised, as farmers or women, even as Dutch soldiers. They take over roadblocks and bridges and telephone exchanges. Radio false orders, and raise all hell with the defences. Some of 'em, they reckon, can speak English better than you or I. But you can always tell the planes that drop 'em. Junkers 52s – the ones with three engines and corrugated wings.' Stan's stomach gave a jump – more sly Jerry dirty tricks.

'Who told you this?' Stan's voice was sharp with fear.

'Why, it's common knowledge, sir. Everyone's talking about it.'

'It's just silly rumours. You know it's against the law to spread worrying rumours. It helps the enemy!' Stan knew he was being pompous, but he couldn't help it.

'Suit yourself,' said the Observer Corps man huffily, and turned his back. Stan stared round gloomily.

'Can I use the binoculars?'

'Suit yourself. They're no damned good for aircraft-spotting – shake all over the blasted sky. I bring me own.' He tapped a smaller pair slung round his neck.

Stan buried his eyes in the great Polish lenses. Twenty-times magnification; they must have been hell to use on the deck of a heaving destroyer. But by God they brought things close. There was the harbour, with its guard-boom and guard-ship; the Castle on its beetling cliff, with the six-inch guns that defended the Gar buried deep in its cliff-face; the beach empty of everything but waves washing through the barbed wire and tank-traps.

Stan sighed comfortably and settled down. It was good to get up here, above things, for a bit. He moved the glasses across the town; it was fun watching people shopping, sweeping pavements, gossiping, not knowing they were being observed. Why, there was the Square, where young McGill lived; at that house with the green door.

Suddenly he stiffened. Maybe this was the way to trace that blasted machine-gun!

The ginger boy had the pistol; it looked odd lying across the copy of *Beano* he was reading.

'*Achtung*!' said Rudi. '*Pistole.*'

The blue eyes flicked up, and the black round eye of the Luger. Rudi put up his hands, and waved the barrel of the gun aside, nervously. The boy watched, a frown on his face.

Rudi tried something else. He mimed pulling a non-existent pistol out of his holster. He pretended to cock it, and then pulled the trigger. He made the noise of a pistol exploding, and traced the bullet ricocheting wildly round the shelter. First he showed it entering his own body, and then the boy's.

'*Tot*. All dead.' The boy looked thoughtful; he was worried about it too.

'See!' said Rudi, and went through the mime of uncocking the pistol, several times, slowly. The boy nodded again, but did nothing. He was wondering if this was some escape attempt. So Rudi went through the mime of tying himself to the bunk by the wrist.

The boy's face brightened; he called something to his friend. The friend came with a bicycle lock and chain. Rudi

130

chained his wrist to the stout upright of the bunk. The boy examined lock and chain closely; he was no fool. Then, gingerly, he tried to uncock the gun, holding it well away from him, eyes screwed tight shut. Rudi sweated; that way it could go off.

'*Nein, nein.* So!' He mimed it over and over again. Finally, after great straining, the boy managed it. He grinned, cocked and uncocked it a dozen times, finally leaving it uncocked. Rudi went through another pantomime with the safety-catch. When that was accomplished they smiled at each other; something attempted, something done. Suddenly they liked each other. The boy pointed at the gun.

'Pistole?' he asked, with a grotesque pronunciation.

'*Pistole,*' Rudi repeated correctly.

'*Pistole*?' said the boy tentatively.

'*Ja Gut,*' said Rudi, and the boy laughed with delight. He pointed to a white enamel mug, lying on the floor.

'*Krug,*' said Rudi. The boy pointed to the hurricane lamp that burnt day and night in the shelter.

'*Sturmlampe,*' said Rudi. Now the other, dark, boy was laughing too. They played the game all the morning, and it was lunch in no time. After that, they played the game every day.

Rudi looked up from the comic.

'*Was ist* Desperate Dan?' His grasp of English was starting to return. If he could make himself word-perfect, it would help his escape when spring came. He was feeling stronger every day now.

'Dan,' said Clogger, pointing at the cartoon of the cowboy; 'Clogger,' pointing to himself; 'Rudi,' pointing at Rudi. The German nodded.

'But "desperate", *was ist das*?' It came out as 'dospreet'.

Clogger rolled his eyes wildly and tore his hair like a madman.

'A nutter?' suggested Rudi.

'Nein . . . no.' Clogger began to pace wildly up and down.

'Ach, yes,' said Rudi, 'but why desperate is he? In these stories he is always winning.' Everybody laughed. Everybody was there. They didn't feel like guards with a prisoner now. More like a class with a teacher, even a family. Especially the little dark one. Every day he sat nearer and nearer to Rudi. Now he was actually leaning against him. There was something wrong with that boy; a terrible need. He moaned in his sleep, and awakened crying. The others were very protective towards him. Where were his parents? Killed in the bombing?

'Give us a song, Rudi,' they chorused. *'Ich hatt' einen kameraden!'*

Rudi obliged. He had a creaky voice, but the confined metal of the shelter helped, like singing in the bath. How long since he'd had a bath?

The children took up the words of the sad old soldiers' song. They sang so sweetly that Rudi was close to tears. What was happening to him? He grew less like a soldier every day; more like a *lehrer* in some kindergarten.

'Hey, belt up you lot,' shouted Clogger. 'Someone might hear us.' They hushed, exchanging furtive glances. Rudi felt part of the plot. Who was on whose side? Had the children no loyalty to the British? Had he any loyalty left to the Germans? If he hadn't been shot down, he'd probably be dead by now. Blown apart in mid-air, or fried, or as full of holes as a colander and every one leaking blood, like some he'd dragged from wreckage.

It was good in the shelter, playing cards, learning English, plenty to eat, if you didn't mind endless corned-beef stew. If only he could have a bath.

Now the children were arguing again. He turned to listen.

'I tell you we *can* make him work. It's in the Geneva Convention.'

'Yah, bollocks. You can't make a prisoner-of-war help you against his own people.'

'You can if it's not war-work. I know a farmer's got two Italians – they were captured in Abyssinia. They mend walls and milk cows and things.'

'Yaah, nuts.'

'Anyway, enlarging the Fortress *is* war-work.'

'Not building a bog and a store-room.'

' 'Tis!'

' 'Tisn't!'

'I quite prepared to build a bog am,' announced Rudi. 'It convenient for me will be too. I do not like going out into the bushes on wet nights. Bogs is not war-work.' It was the longest speech he had ever made in English. They looked startled.

'Wot kind of bog?'

'Oh, the very best kind, I you assure. As they had on farms when I a boy was. Mit a seat and bucket, and holder for the paper.'

'We'd have to keep you fastened up by one ankle!'

'That will be in order.' And so the bog was built. The only underground bombproof bog in the country, they informed each other, except for the King's and Winston Churchill's. The children produced heavy oak doors from the Nichol house, and a bucket and sandbags; and Rudi enjoyed getting his shirt off and sweating in the early April sun.

When it was finished, and joined to everything else by a covered trench, even Audrey agreed it was all right. She said her granny who lived in the country had one, and said they were All Right if Properly Aired and Seen To Regularly.

'A ventilator, so,' said Rudi proudly, patting the sand-bagged opening on top, 'and to it I will see every morning. But not with this great drainpipe tied to my ankle, no!'

'Sorry, Rudi,' they said, and untied him. They still carried round the pistol, uncocked; but they often left it lying carelessly on one side these days. Rudi fancied he could have reached it, twice, but somehow . . . it would have spoilt the building of the bog. And it was a good well-made bog.

'What other thing can I make that not War Effort is?' asked Rudi. And building, as the April days lengthened and no enemies, either British or German, came, was all their joy. The Fortress became an intricate network of trenches, tunnels and underground bunkers that threatened to rival the Maginot Line. The children, Rudi could only assume, became better and better thieves. Daily they dumped bricks, doors, windows and even coils of barbed wire at Rudi's feet. Rudi did his best with the wire, but he was no infantryman. He stretched it (tangled into the briars and bushes) all round the Fortress.

'Ah, well,' said Chas, 'it will keep Boddser Brown out.' Chas spent his days carefully lettering two signs to hang on the wire. One for the back, to keep out the British, read WAR DEPARTMENT. NO ADMITTANCE. And one for the front (just behind the concealing fence) which had a skull and crossbones and read ACHTUNG MINEN! Everyone, including Rudi, pronounced them very effective.

'It scare me silly would, if I a poor soldier were!'

The little dark boy laughed, and thrust his arm through Rudi's. 'That's good, Dad!'

'Hey, Rudi, were you *really* a fighter pilot?'

'*Ja!*'

'And shot down two Spitfires?' Rudi groaned; they didn't want *that* story again, did they?

'Well, how come you got out of your plane alive; the guns were still firing when it blew up.'

'I tell you a secret. That day I was having a joy-ride with a friend. I observer was.'

'Rear-gunner,' said Chas starkly. 'Messerschmitt 110s don't carry an observer; they carry a rear-gunner.'

'So . . .?' Rudi knew what was coming.

'So you could mend our machine-gun if you wanted to.'

'Ha,' said Rudi. He'd have been scared of them once, but not now. 'What will you do to me if I do not mend it?'

'We could shoot you,' said Chas.

'I the Geneva Convention plead. Prisoners-of-war are never shot.'

'That's right!' shouted everyone indignantly, turning on Chas.

'Well . . . we could hand you over to the Army!'

Rudi laughed.

'So many questions they would ask. Interrogate me with rubber hoses and bright lights, like in the American movies. I spill the beans might.' Everybody laughed.

Then Clogger said, 'We do want the gun mended though. It's important.' Everyone looked at Rudi solemnly. He wriggled uncomfortably. It would be wrong to give children back a gun like that. Because they *were* still children. But somehow, he couldn't insult them by *saying* that. Because, in another way, they were no longer children.

'We wouldn't fire it, promise. Except at . . .' Chas paused and blushed; he had almost forgotten that Rudi was a German. 'Anyway, we wouldn't fire it, just . . . have it. It's our mascot.'

What could Rudi say, to save their face? He thought long.

'I do you a deal. I need a boat. You a sailing boat get – I the gun will mend.' It was, he thought, the right thing to say, adult to adult. They couldn't possibly *get* a boat.

135

TWELVE

'Damn this for a game of soldiers,' thought Stan Liddell. He couldn't feel his feet, they were so cold. He couldn't stop the great binoculars shaking. A fortnight, off and on, he'd watched the house in the Square, the one with the green door. Often he'd seen young McGill come out, always with that wary glance round as he left the garden gate. For a fortnight no policeman had tried to shadow the boy; but he was wary by instinct now, like a wild animal.

The binoculars had been a disappointment. Things got in their way: houses, hedges, factory chimneys. Sometimes, when the boy vanished behind them, Stan could guess which way he was going; but sooner or later, when he vanished for the third or fourth time, he vanished for good. And Stan had to hand it to him; in all the time he'd watched, he'd never seen the boy go the same way twice.

This morning, there was a difference; there *was* someone following. Stan swore. Could these policemen never let well alone?

Then he saw it wasn't a policeman, but someone quite different. Stan knew two things straight away. McGill had immediately become aware of being followed, though he didn't look round. And the someone different was up to no good. Stan suddenly felt colder than ever, and afraid. Should he rush down and interfere? But how could he hope to catch them? They were a quarter-of-a-mile away already. Hopelessly, Stan continued to watch through his binoculars.

Faffing fool! thought Chas. Does he think I don't know he's there. He walked extra-quiet, listening to the footsteps behind. They were too light for Fatty Hardy, and that sergeant limped. But the feet wore boots with heelplates; some eager young copper perhaps.

Chas grinned with glee. Let's see how good this one is! Let's see if he can get through a hawthorn hedge without snagging his nice serge trousers. Let's see if he can cross a glass-topped wall without tearing his backside out!

Chas dawdled along to the hawthorn hedge. There were only two gaps in it, hidden by dead-nettles. Chas walked past the first, and suddenly wriggled through the second. Once through, he ran back silently to the first. He peered through it; a pair of large black boots was just vanishing through the second. Chas scrambled back into the road, and streaked off the way he had come. By the time the copper found the second hole, he'd be a mile away.

But half-a-minute later, the boots were behind him again. Chas slowed to a walk, saying good-morning with great innocence to a friend of his mother's who was pushing her pram. So he was a *smart* copper, this one!

Chas tried him on the glass-topped wall; but the copper was equally good at walls. So Chas gave him the water-pipe that spanned the Red Burn. The Red Burn was only a foot deep, but full of a peculiar (and staining) red mud. And the water-pipe was stickily tarred and only six inches wide. Chas always ran over it (you kept your balance if you ran fast enough) but coppers always lost their nerve, and tried sitting astride. Joy of joys, they often got stuck in the middle.

But this copper crossed the pipe on his feet.

'Must be Scotland Yard,' muttered Chas, getting flustered. They would be expecting him at the Fortress; he was already half-an-hour late. 'Right, I'll give him the Mud

Flats, then.' Chas had kept the mud-flats in reserve until now; they were a vast swamp by the river below the town, covered at this season with dead white reeds four feet high, and crossed by black oozing streams that sported the unhealthy rainbows of oil-patches. What paths there were, crossed the streams by sodden rotten planks. They were only used by anglers and small boys, and you had to know them well, for they were the terror of all local mothers; children had drowned there in the past.

The Flats were only two hundred yards from the Nichol house. I'll be drinking my tea in ten minutes, thought Chas. He ran across the first bridge, ducked and sped sharp left. Crouching low, he changed direction six more times and then crouched on a dry patch under the skeleton of a wrecked fishing-boat. He then realised uneasily that he'd put himself in a cul-de-sac. There was no way out from the wrecked boat except the way he'd come. Still, he *must* have lost the policeman pretty thoroughly by this time.

He started to giggle, and then stifled it. Footsteps were squelching towards him, searching carefully. In another second they'd be on him. Was it a policeman at all? He realised what a lonely place he had chosen. Only fishermen ever came here, and they only came on Sundays in summer.

Rudi wakened and looked at his watch. They had all slept in this morning. Last night the boys had been overexcited, whispering. Rudi had heard the town clock chime one, through the black-out, before he'd dropped off.

Clogger was snoring in the top bunk, loud enough to keep the flies away. Rudi glanced at the bottom bunk, where his guard always sat, and gasped. His moment had come: the moment of weakness he had predicted; and, also as he'd predicted, it had come via the little dark boy.

138

Nicky lay full-length on the bottom bunk, right arm outstretched, fingers closed loosely round the Luger. The pistol lay on the rough tartan rug not two feet from Rudi's nose. Rudi slipped his wrist out of the cycle-chain that should have fastened him to the bunk; he'd perfected that trick weeks ago. He leaned over and took hold of the Luger barrel with two fingers, and began to draw it gently towards him. Nicky's finger was just sliding off the trigger when he moaned and tightened his grip.

Rudi waited; for he saw, with a slight shudder, that the foolish nervous one had the gun cocked again, and the safety-catch off.

The footsteps squelched nearer. What was it that was following him? A convict, a murderer? One of the Undead that Cem said lived in graveyards? Or one of those awful strange men his mother was constantly warning him never to speak to? Why mustn't one speak to them, or take the sweets they always offered you? His mother would never say. If he asked his father, Mr McGill always just shuffled his *Daily Express* angrily and told him to shut his bloody yap.

A head was emerging over the reeds. The sun was behind it, and he could see no more than two protruding ears. The being stopped and looked at Chas.

In a second, all his wild imaginings flew away, and a much worse fear took their place. The being was Boddser Brown.

Gently, Rudi tried again. This time the child didn't even moan. The German uncocked the gun, put on the safety-catch, and returned it to its rightful place in his holster. Both boys slept on.

What now? Should he simply walk out? But that would

mean no more food, no more tramp-disguise (for his sacks had long since been put to other use). Besides, the moment they awakened, the children would warn the *polizei* and the army. They'd comb the whole area; he wouldn't get a mile.

Slince the children? He couldn't bear to harm them, and tying them up would do no good. In an hour the others would arrive and release them. Wait till they were all here, and tie them all up? He doubted his ability to tie up six in a way that would last half-an-hour.

Use the gun to take charge of the Fortress? Hold all six permanent prisoners? Water would soon run out, and besides four of them would have to return home by dark. Missing children would start a bigger hue and cry than any German airman on the run.

The more he racked his brains, the more impossible it seemed. Besides, he realized sadly, he just didn't want to escape. His patriotism towards the Fatherland was dead. He tried to coax it back to life: thought of the Fuehrer; thought of his old father and mother and how ashamed they'd be of his cowardice. What would the neighbours back home say? I'd be shot as a deserter if the Fuehrer knew, he mused.

But his parents, and neighbours and the Fuehrer would never know. At home, by now, he would be a dead hero; his photograph in uniform, draped in black, would be on his mother's mantelpiece, a source of pride.

Meanwhile, it was drizzling steadily outside, and he wanted his breakfast. Better a live jackal than a dead lion. But he had the advantage of being both at once! He couldn't help laughing.

It remained to save the little dark boy's pride. He slid the Luger back, just as carefully, between the outstretched fingers. Then he slid his wrist back through the chain, and yawned loudly. Through his lowered lashes, he watched Nicky awaken, and grab frantically at the gun.

'I'm hungry!' announced Rudi.

'Och, Ah could eat a horse too,' said Clogger, stretching. 'Ma turn to make the tea.'

Rudi smiled. Life was good.

Chas looked round desperately, but there was no way out except the path Boddser Brown stood astride. Nor was there anything to hit Boddser with. He wrenched at a rib of the old boat, but his hand just slipped on the oozing wood. Next minute he was lying face-down on the wet grass with one arm twisted behind his back, and Boddser's knee on his neck. He twisted his head, for black water was getting into his nostrils and mouth.

'Gerroff, you swine,' he snarled; it was a gesture without hope.

'Poor old Chassy McGill,' crooned Boddser, with evil sentimentality. 'Where's your brains now, Chas?' He twisted Chas's arm up tighter. 'Why don't you shout for help? Go on, shout.'

Chas shouted. It couldn't do any harm.

'Louder!' Boddser twisted Chas's arm tighter. 'Louder!' He gave another twist. 'Louder!'

Nobody came.

'Right, to business,' said Boddser briskly, moving his knee from Chas's neck to the small of his back. 'Where's that machine-gun?'

'Sod off,' gasped Chas. He gave a vigorous squirm that half threw Boddser off, and crawled for dear life. But it only made things worse. He was now hanging face down over a little black stream. And he knew what was coming next.

'Thank you, McGill,' said Boddser. 'That's saved me a

lot of trouble.' Chas took a deep breath and closed his mouth as his head was thrust under water. He was under a long time, while his chest swelled and swelled until it felt it would burst. Then his head was released. He breathed out. He felt Bodser's hand coming down to push him under again before he could breath in. He moved his head quickly and Boddser's hand slipped. Chas snatched a breath before he went under again. He felt strangely calm.

THIRTEEN

AFTER half-an-hour, Boddser began to get worried. Things were not turning out as usual. Usually, by this time, kids were blubbing, begging for mercy, willing to do anything; which made Boddser feel hot and good and squelchy inside, and then he'd let the kids go.

But McGill wasn't like that. He just went on spitting out swear-words, whenever he had the breath. And once, when Boddser's hand had slipped, McGill had bitten his wrist hard and savage, like a dog. Boddser stared fascinated at the horse-shoe of teethmarks in his own precious flesh. They hurt; they seeped blood into the muddy wetness of his arm. Boddser started to fret. The dirty water might turn the wound septic.

And now McGill lay silent, motionless, breathing in a funny sort of way. Had he fainted, or had a fit? He had acted so queerly. But Boddser gave his arm a twist.

'Want some more, McGill?' There was no response. Boddser got to his feet, suddenly shaking, terrified. What had he done?

Next minute, McGill was up and gone, running now like a small muddy rat. Boddser roared with rage and pursued. Fooled again!

McGill crossed the first plank-bridge and seemed to fall. 'Got you!' roared Boddser and made to cross the plank. Chas twisted round, caught the end of the plank and threw it into the water. Boddser, unable to stop, went into the stream up to his waist. The coldness of the water made him gasp. By the time he'd scrambled out, McGill had crossed the next plank and thrown that in the water too. Boddser gathered himself and crossed the stream in one gigantic leap. McGill ran for his life.

He was catching him now! In fact, he'd stopped, with his back against a fence. Why, that was the old bombed-out Nichol house behind. What was the little rat shouting? Clogger? Why was he shouting Clogger?

'So we start again, McGill. Where's that machine-gun?'

'No, we won't. Look behind you!'

'Think I'd fall for that trick, stupid?.'

'Perhaps ye'd better,' said a new voice behind him. Boddser whirled.

'Clogger Duncan! But you went home to Glasgow!'

'Some people thought Ah did,' said Clogger grimly. 'What shall we do with him, Chas?'

'He's been torturing me, to get me to tell about the gun.'

'Och, he has, has he?'

'Now wait,' said Boddser, backing away. 'It's none of your business, Duncan. It was a fair fight, one against one.'

'When did you fight fair?' said Clogger. He turned to Chas. 'It's up to you, Chas. We can't afford this lad any more. Shall I do him proper?' Chas didn't even think. He was black with hate.

'Do him proper,' he said.

It had been a fair fight. There had even been a time when Clogger's nose had streamed red, and Chas thought, horrors upon horrors, that he might lose. But Clogger cared no more for his bleeding nose than a fly. He just kept on and on, white, silent, steady as a man chopping wood. He never touched Boddser's face; always hit his body where it wouldn't show. And Boddser was much too keen not to get hurt.

So, in the end, Boddser was lying on the ground being very sick. Chas watched fascinated as the green strings of slime trailed from his mouth.

'Had enough?' asked Clogger. Boddser nodded silently. 'Aye, ye've had enough for now. Enough till ye get home and blab to your mother that I'm still here in Garmouth, and where I'm living, and that Chas knows all about it. You know where the machine-gun is now, don't you? *And* your precious mother'll run straight to the police.'

Boddser's eyes flickered. Clogger had read his thoughts exactly. 'They'll send you away to Borstal,' he managed to mumble. '*All* of you.'

'If you tell them.'

'Try and stop me!'

'Ah will!' Clogger raised his boot and kicked Boddser in the ribs three times. It made a terrible noise, like a butcher chopping a leg of lamb. Then he kicked him three times more, and three times more. Boddser was much more sick now. When he looked up, his eyes had changed. He looked as if he understood something he had never understood before ...

'Ye can put me in Borstal,' said Clogger, 'but you can't keep me there. Ah'll get out, and when Ah do, Ah'll come looking for you, Brown. And Ah'll finish off what I started the day. Ye understand me, Brown? Ah'll kill you, if Ah swing for it.'

Boddser believed him. Chas, staring in horror, believed him too. This was a Clogger he had never known existed; a Clogger he had called out.

They left Boddser lying, and walked back to the camp in silence. Somehow, the silence went before them. Cem, Audrey and Carrot-juice just sat and stared. Rudi, pretending to read, watched round a corner of *Beano*.

'Ah'll wash ma face!' said Clogger loudly, to no one in particular. Audrey poured out hot water without a word.

145

Clogger carefully cleaned the dark cracked blood off his mouth and chin. Then he looked up at Chas.

'Ye didnae like that, did ye? So ye'll no be speaking to me any more. You've nae time for Glasgow hooligans.' Chas neither looked up nor spoke. He drew, in the dust of the floor, with the toe of his wellington boot.

'D'you want to go running to the poliss about me as well?' Silence. 'It was you who said to do him proper.'

'I didn't know what doing him proper *meant*.'

'Ye didnae think it meant gieing him a clout on the ear and sending him bawling to his ma? Ye didnae want the poliss round here in an hour, did ye?' Chas shook his head mutely.

'Then what other way would *ye* have shut his trap?' Chas shook his head mutely again.

'Och, you're nobbut a bairn.'

'I'm *not* a bairn. He ducked my head under water for half an hour and I told him *nothing*.'

Clogger walked across to Chas and, tipping his head back by the hair, examined him closely. Chas was as white as a sheet with great black rings around his eyes. Clogger let go his hair and ruffled it with great affection.

'God, man, ye're half-drowned. Aye, Ah guess you're a hard man in your own way, Chassy McGill. Hard on yerself.' Chas felt a hot traitor tear start in the corner of his left eye. It was the admiration in Clogger's voice he couldn't bear.

'Oh, let's have a cup of tea,' he said. 'I'm O.K.' He proved it by being splendidly sick for the next quarter-of-an-hour.

Stan Liddell knocked on Chas's front door. Mrs McGill opened it.

'Why hello, Mr Liddell! Do you want Charles? You'll

have to go up to the bedroom I'm afraid. He came home in a right muck last night – thick wi' mud and soaked to the skin. He can't raise his arms above his head this morning, and he look's like someone's been at his eyes wi' a blackin' brush. Expect he's been fighting again – you know what lads are.'

Half-an-hour later, Stan knocked on Boddser Brown's front door.

'Mr Liddell,' said Mrs Brown. 'I was just thinking of calling the police, but you'll do as well. Bernard came home in a shocking state last night – soaked to the skin and plastered with mud from head to foot. He's been crying all morning – I've had the doctor to him. You should see his poor little ribs – they're black and blue. He won't say a word, but a mother *knows* – it's those big lads been at him again – that Charles McGill. I don't know what the world's coming to, with all this hooliganism . . . you should just see his bruises, poor mite . . .' She went on for a very long time, saying the same things over and over again. Finally Stan gave her a look that stopped her dead.

'I wouldn't advise the police, madam. I've just come from McGill's house, and he's in just the same state. What's more, you're son's far bigger than McGill, and I happen to know he started the business . . .' Stan was amazed how sharp his voice was; he supposed it was the permanent whine in Mrs Brown's voice, her permanent conviction that the world would always do her and hers down, the mingy look on her face . . .

But it wasn't her face that Stan remembered as he walked home for tea; it was the two boys' faces. McGill as pale as death, but oddly triumphant; Brown cowering and hopeless. It was easy to guess who'd won the fight. But there was more to it than that, something that Stan couldn't put his finger on.

Both boys, of course, shut up like clams when he mentioned their injuries. Ah, well, thought Stan, at least I know they haven't killed each other. Then he went back to worrying about German paratroopers.

FOURTEEN

NICKY was as stubborn as a mule.

'I never went sailing with my father before the War!'

'Yes you did,' said Cem. 'You used to boast about it at school. And I saw you out with him once. It was a boat with a red sail!'

'He hired that from a fisherman.'

'No he didn't. You told me he had his own boathouse on the river.'

'It got bombed,' said Nicky stubbornly.

'Where *was* it, then?' Everyone stared at Nicky in silence; he fidgeted a long time.

'All right, it's still there. At Prior's Haven. But the key to the boathouse got lost when our house was bombed.'

'Where was it kept?' asked Clogger. 'We'll find it!'

They searched the ruined kitchen half the day. At last, Clogger straightened his back, groaned wearily and said, 'It is lost, Ah reckon. We'll have tey force the lock on the boathouse door.'

'It's all right,' muttered Nicky. 'I've got the key here.' He reached down into his shirt and pulled up a key on a string.

'For hell's sake, what's the matter with ye?' roared Clogger. 'Are ye part of this gang or no?'

'It's my boat,' said Nicky. 'It's my father's boat.' He began to snivel. Clogger stared at him.

'Aye, well, in that case I'll be away home to Glasgow the morrow. Ah can't afford to hang round here all ma life. Ye can have the Fortress, Nicky, all of it. That's yours as well. And you can sort out Rudi as you think fit. Ah'll be

149

packing ma things.' Nicky looked round the others for support. They all stared at the floor. Nicky suddenly felt alone, and very frightened.

'Sorry, Nicky,' said Chas, 'but we've got to give Rudi that boat, 'cos otherwise he won't mend that gun. And the Germans are coming soon, and we'll need it.'

'Who says the Germans are coming?'

'My dad. He says if they don't come soon, they won't be able to come, and then they'll have to admit they've lost the War.' There was a murmur of assent.

'Everyone knows they're coming.'

'The soldiers dug pits on our soccer field to make their gliders crash.'

'The BBC said vicars had to ring the churchbells when they came.'

'Oh, all right,' said Nicky, hopelessly. 'What do you want me to do?'

'Take us and show us where the boat is,' said Chas, embarrassed.

'But I can't go out. People will recognize me!'

'Not in a balaclava helmet they won't. You'll pass for a slum kid. You're mucky enough.'

The boathouse lock was rusty, but Clogger had brought an oil-can and it yielded at last. They passed into a gloom that smelt of tar, rope and stale water. They pulled the door shut behind them, and there was only light from a little window high up.

Half the place was filled with the licking smacking waters of the river; the other half was full of white boat, yellow masts and red sails.

There was a packet of Capstan cigarettes on the side-bench, falling apart and brown with damp. Nicky could remember his father putting it there. Halfway home in the car, his father had remembered that packet of Capstans, left behind on the bench. But he'd said, 'Never mind, we'll pick them up the next time we sail.' There never had been a next time.

'My mother never came here,' said Nicky, staring at the cigarettes. 'She said sailing was a man's thing.' The other two boys shuffled awkwardly.

'Ah see the boat's outa the water.' Clogger hefted the boat's weight.

'Yes, that stops her rotting in winter.'

'Ah reckon we can manage her. Gies a hand, lads.' Slowly they edged the boat in. Chas was clumsy, and the stone of the jetty scraped the dinghy's white paint. Nicky felt it was his own heart that was being scraped. But in it went.

'Och, it's filling up wi' water!' said Clogger in disgust. 'It's no good. It's rotted.'

'No, no,' cried Nicky, 'it's just that the planks have shrunk apart, from getting so dry. Leave her sunk a day and the seams will close and she'll be fine. She always does that.' The next moment, he could have bitten his tongue out. He'd had a chance to save his boat, but now it was too late.

'Can we fit the mast and ropes and things?' asked Chas, curious. 'Best to do it now – we mightn't have another chance before Rudi goes.'

So, with heavy-hearted skill, Nicky showed them how; while all the while, just over his shoulder, his father seemed to watch disapprovingly.

They went back the next day, and the next. And, dashing Nicky's last hope, the seams of the dinghy did close and it became watertight. They loaded everything useful in; Audrey added a gallon can of water and some tins of food. Chas brought his own compass. Everything was as ready as it ever could be.

151

FIFTEEN

It was not yet midnight, and already it was the worst raid of the war. The door-curtain of the Anderson was framed a ghastly orange-pink, and even a mile from the river they could smell the burning oil.

'They've got the Docks this time,' announced Mrs Spalding with mournful satisfaction.

Anti-aircraft guns barked on and on, like a pack of cheated hounds. There were more of them than there used to be, but they weren't making much difference. Chas watched fragments of cork dropping off the shelter wall. He counted them as they lay on the floor. Anything to keep his mind off things. His mother was knitting with great calmness; that was always a bad sign. Mrs Spalding had her ear perilously close to the door-curtain, ready to retail the latest piece of bad news as it was shouted from shelter to shelter.

'Ashington's been hit; there's fifty men trapped by a bomb down the Rising Sun Colliery.

'South Shields gas holder's been hit; it's burning.' Then, with a sudden squeak of real fear in her voice, she said, 'What's that?' They all listened; nothing but bombs and guns. Silly stupid bitch, thought Chas. Haven't we got enough trouble, without inventing more?

'What did you *think* you heard, Mrs Spalding?' asked Mrs McGill icily. She didn't hold with such hysterical goings-on.

'I thought perhaps I heard the church-bells ringing.'

'Perhaps someone's getting married,' giggled Chas. Then his heart froze. For, in a lull of the guns they suddenly all heard the bells, sweet with overtones of Sunday morning and Christmas. But that was long ago. Now bells meant ...

Invasion. In Chas's mind's eye they came: the hard-faced hordes in their coal-scuttle helmets; the crawling irresistible Panzers; the lines of Stukas like straight bars across the sky. All his childhood they had stormed through the cinema newsreels, jackbooting triumphantly through Vienna, Prague, Warsaw, Paris. Now they would jackboot through Garmouth. Followed by the Gestapo. Knocks on your door, people dragged away in the middle of the night, firing-squads.

A traitorous voice awakened in Chas's mind. If you behaved yourself, if you didn't resist, if you made friends with them ... a hand clutched his stomach tighter and tighter as the adults sat silent and the shelter filled with the queer smell of fear.

'It must be some mistake,' said Mrs McGill, tight-lipped.

Nobody answered.

'It came from up Blyth way,' said Mrs Spalding. 'There's plenty of the army up there to deal with them.' Again, nobody answered.

The clutching hand was spreading from Chas's stomach. It was groping between his legs now. You couldn't make friends with the Gestapo, any more than you could with diphtheria or scarlet fever germs; they were not human. And he *wouldn't* sit here with the adults, shaking, waiting to be slaughtered like cattle.

He wanted to fight and die ... it suddenly seemed good and clean to fight and be dead; the Gestapo couldn't get hold of you once you were dead ... there was the gun ... the gun ... the gun. He swallowed and controlled his breath; he must seem calm.

'Mum, I want to go to the lav.'

'Not now.' His mother opened and shut her mouth like a rat-trap.

'But Mum, I'll wet myself. And it's a lull, Mum. No bombers. The Germans aren't here yet ... I'd better go while I can ... Mum, I'm bursting.'

'All right, go,' screamed his mother. Chas climbed out of the shelter carefully, because his knees were shaking; he walked calmly down the garden path towards the lav. He even remembered to open the lav door and close it with a bang, like he always did. Then he was streaking down the back garden, past his dad's greenhouse. There was a half-moon and he could see the rabbits in their hutches, peacefully eating the dandelion leaves he had gathered that morning, a million years ago.

He stopped ... the rabbits ... they deserved their chance too. When the Germans came they would wring their necks and eat them for sure ... He turned back. He opened the greenhouse door and then the hutch-doors one by one. The rabbits leapt down and onto the moonlit lawn, sniffing curiously at their newfound freedom.

And then Chas was gone through the bushes, running for the Fortress.

'What can we *do*?' cried Mrs Jones, wringing her hands ineffectually.

'Oh, those storm-troopers, they *rape* young girls,' said Miss Jones breathlessly, hugging her small and neat bosom protectively, as if the SS were already on the doorstep.

But old Cemetery Jones stood as firm as a rock.

'I've been getting ready for this day a long time,' he said heavily. 'It's taken thought, but I've done it, *and* no one the wiser. Come on, missus, fetch your valuables; come on you kids, fetch those blankets.'

'Where are you going, Cecil, are you mad?'

'We're going to t'graveyard, woman.' Mrs Jones shrieked, but Cemetery Senior took her hand firmly and led her out of the Anderson, round the Cemetery Lodge and out among the tombstones. The guns were silent, the bells still chimed, the moon rode high, and the angels on the graves flickered white as they passed. Cem and his sister followed with the blankets, mesmerized.

A larger bulk loomed up; a marble block as big as a garage, with white ionic columns and marble urns on top. It had a huge bronze double-door.

'The Irving Tomb,' announced old Cemetery, in his best undertaker's tones. 'Those doors is best bronze and three inches thick, and the marble's best quality and two foot thick. Stop a howitzer, that would.' He fished in his pocket and produced an elaborate bronze key which he thrust into the double door.

'But,' screamed Mrs Jones, 'what about them dead Irvings?'

'Moved them in with the Ibbotsons three months ago. People must learn to accept smaller accommodation in an emergency. I've got it very nice in there, missus. Just as you like it. Bit of carpet on the floor; mattresses on the slabs instead of coffins ... plenty of tinned-food, even a picture on the wall.'

'God love us,' said Mrs Jones, and let herself be guided in by the light of his torch. 'I suppose it's better than the Germans.'

An old damp smell came out of the tomb, and tickled the end of Cem's nose. He didn't like it, didn't like it at all. Fastened up in the dark, not knowing what was happening outside ... and that smell ... in the end he didn't make any decision. His legs started working of their own accord. Suddenly he was running for the cemetery wall, hurdling gravestones and flowerpots like some Olympic sprinter. Heading for the Fortress.

'Come back, you young fool!' shouted Cem Senior,

155

waving his torch around in increasingly wide arcs. But he was no sprinter, and his son had vanished. He still had two to care for, and two *was* more important than one. He went back to his wife, muttering.

'Young fool, just when I had everything so nice and *comfortable.*'

'Daddy, where *are* we going?' asked Audrey.

'Shut up and get those garage doors open.' Mr Parton was panting, even before he began pulling the starting-handle of the big black car.

'But where are we going, Daddy?' Mr Parton swore a string of oaths previously unheard by his family.

'Stop that language in front of the children, Bertie,' said his wife, already comfortably settled in the back of the car. In her best fur coat she almost filled the back seat. Her arms were full of hatboxes. Young Bertie peeped from under her elbow, white-faced and open-mouthed but wearing his school cap.

'Shut up, you stupid cow,' roared Mr Parton, swinging on the starting-handle like a dervish. The car jerked into back-firing life.

'Right, in.' Mr Parton flung Audrey roughly into the front passenger seat and slammed the car-door shut. He got behind the wheel and fumbled for the car-lights button in the dark; the windscreen-wipers started working.

'Daddy, where *are* we going?'

'To your Aunt Emily's in Westmorland.'

'But why?'

'Because the faffing Germans are coming, that's why.'

'You mean the Invasion?'

'Well, I don't mean flaming Guy Fawkes' Night.' The car jolted out of the garage and turned left too sharply, scraping the offside wing on the gatepost.

'But Winston Churchill said we were to stay put if the Germans invaded. Otherwise we'd block the roads for the Army, like the French refugees did.'

'Damn Winston Churchill. He's safe enough. He'll be flying to Canada now, with the Royal Family. He doesn't care about us, so why should we care about him?'

'But nobody else is leaving!'

'Well they ain't got cars, have they? They ain't got petrol. Eight quid for eight gallons that cost me on the Black Market. That's a week's wages.'

'But Daddy, we're *running away.*'

'Shut up, will you.' The car took a corner dangerously, on two wheels. Audrey looked out miserably. She liked doing what was right; and this wasn't. It wasn't patriotic, either. How would she face her friends at school when it was all over? The Partons the only family who ran away? Her friends . . . the Fortress!

'Stop, Daddy, look, look!' There was a squeal of brakes, and the car stopped with a suddenness that shot Mrs Parton and her hatboxes painfully forward.

'What the hell . . .' shouted Parton. But the door on Audrey's side was swinging open, and she was gone.

She ran and ran, not looking where she was going, but *not* running away from the enemy. She ran till she tripped and fell, then lay low. In the distance, she could hear her father shouting and swearing at her; it sounded as if now he really hated her. She kept silent, tears in her eyes that were not from her fall.

Her father called and called. But finally she heard the car doors slam and the car move away.

She got up, and realized where she was. Limping and sobbing, she headed for the Fortress.

In the Brownlee shelter, Mrs Ridley sat keeping an eye

on Mrs Brownlee, and Mrs Brownlee sat keeping an eye on her son John.

'He's badly, tonight,' said Mrs Brownlee. John's green eyes roved round and round the shelter, never stopping for a minute. His great hands wrestled with each other, over and over. Every so often he would start to his feet, and it took all the women's efforts to make him sit down.

They had tried all the usual ways to pacify him; cups of tea, sandwiches. But even his favourite penny lollipops had little effect. Two lay half-sucked on the floor. It was like being fastened up with a terrified elephant.

Mrs Ridley was afraid of the Germans. Mrs Brownlee was afraid of what the Germans would do to her son when they caught him. She knew very well what had happened to mental defectives in Germany; one lethal injection solved the problem.

John was simply afraid. He could smell the fear in the air, his mother's fear. But he could never understand where the fear was coming from. He could no more understand about tanks and stormtroopers and bombers than he could have understood a maths problem. To him, the whole world had become terrifying. Like an animal, he wanted to run and bury himself in a black hole. But he didn't have a black hole to run to.

Another bomb dropped, very close. It did no harm to the shelter, but it burst the sandbags that protected the shelter door like paper-bags. The earth from them trickled through the door, under the blackout curtain, and formed a little pile on the floor.

John reached forward and began to shovel it out again with his hands. As he did so, it triggered off a memory. There was another shelter where he had shovelled earth with his hands – but that shelter had been full of laughter and fun and children who were kind. That was the safe place he must run to now.

He reared up to his great height and put a foot out of the door. Outside, the guns took up their furious song, and clouds of shrapnel whistled down.

'No, John, no!'

'Where you going? Come back!' The two small women flung themselves onto him. But he roared and flung them off.

'Where you going now?' he roared in triumph, and was gone. Mrs Brownlee picked herself up.

'Don't go out there, love,' gasped Mrs Ridley.

'I've got to. He'll hurt himself.'

At the end of the Square, John paused. He didn't know where the marvellous happy shelter was. And then he saw something shining on a doorstep ahead. Somebody had put out their milk-bottles for the morning. John knew he had to pick up the bottles; that was the way to the happy place. Pick up the milk-bottles and follow the boy round to the right, and then turn left. John thundered on.

And after him, terrified but faithful, Mrs Brownlee followed at a distance.

'Chas! CHASSY!' Mrs McGill wandered from room to room of her darkened house. An answering call came from the front upstairs bedroom. She opened the door. Two figures sat by the open window, in silhouette against the circling searchlights.

'Chassy?' The figures turned.

'No, it's me and Granda, love.' It was Nana.

'What you doing? Why aren't you down the shelter?' Mrs McGill nearly lost control of her voice, and regained it with an effort.

'Granda and me's waiting for the Jarmans, hinny. Ah've

159

got the breadknife and he's got the carving-knife. And I've got me bottles handy.' She pointed to a row of pop-bottles on the windowsill.

'What's in those?'

'Oil of vitriol, hinny. That'll burn their thieving faces off. Ah can just reach them if I throw from here.'

'But they'll shoot you!'

'Aye well, they can shoot us both together. Forty years we've had, and they're not separating us into those consecration camps at our age. We'll go together, sink or swim.'

Granda coughed, rackingly.

'Hey, man, wrap yourself up better. You'll catch your death.' Nana rearranged the mufflers round his neck, and straightened his cap.

'You should be in bed, Granda,' said Mrs McGill.

'Nay, lass. Ah'll face them buggers on me feet, like Ah always did.'

'Chassy's run off somewhere. I can't find him. He said he was going to the lav, but he's gone. And he's let his rabbits out all over the garden. I can't catch them. They're eating all the spring-cabbages.'

'He'll be off to the fighting, mevve,' said Nana placidly. 'McGills always went to the fighting young. Granda here volunteered to fight the Boers when he was only sixteen.'

'Oh, Nana, he *can't* have!' Mrs McGill was screeching now.

'Rest yourself, hinny. If the Jarmans don't come, he'll be home by morning. And if they do, he'll have as much chance as anybody else ...' She settled herself comfortably. She was wearing her best hat and coat, because the Jarmans were riff-raff and had to be kept in their place.

Mrs McGill ran downstairs. Where could she look? What should she do?

SIXTEEN

IT was a wild scene from the top of Billing's Mill. Clouds boiled across the moon; and black smoke boiled, lower and in a different direction, across the clouds. Three Observer Corps were on duty. One side of their steel helmets gleamed blue with the moon, and the other side red with fire.

Stan Liddell, more than anyone in Garmouth, could see what was happening. The Dock fires were spreading; the tall black cranes stood out in silhouette. A pink flush to the north would be Blyth, and a fainter glow to the west would be Newcastle burning.

Below him, the mill was plunged in darkness. Had a bomb knocked out the electricity cables, or was there sabotage? Why had the searchlights at the Castle suddenly gone out, half-an-hour ago? He felt the solid reassurance of Sandy move up behind him.

'All small-arms issued, sar. All personnel have reported and been sent to their place of duty.'

Stan reached for the left-hand phone – a landline to the single concrete pillbox that guarded the Coast Road Bridge, a mile away.

'Allo, allo, allo!'

'For God's sake, Sergeant Mullins, answer the phone correctly.'

'Sorry, sir. Number One post here, sir.'

'Everyone arrived?'

'All but Wansdyke, sir. Wait on, sir. He's just turned up, sir.'

'Got your pickets out?'

'Yessir.'

'Anything moving?'

'One or two cars tried to cross the bridge – civvy refugees sir. Turned 'em back, sir. But they're just going round by the other road. Any news your end, sir?'

'Nothing. Keep alert.'

'Yessir.' The sergeant was reluctant to go; he sounded pretty lonely. Stan rang Number Two post, a sandbagged cottage over the Docks.

'Pretty hot down here, sir. Nothing moving but fire-brigade and rescue.' Number Three post, on the coast north of the Castle, reported an empty beach. Stan tried to ring the military at the Castle; the female operator said all the lines to the Castle were in use. She was half-hysterical but shouting at her only made her worse. Was she really hysterical or faking it? She sounded a bit foreign. When Stan asked her where she came from she said Gateshead and burst into tears. Only the tears didn't sound like real tears. Oh, hell, thought Stan, I'll be imagining German paratroopers under my bed next.

'Why not try Royal Navy, Blyth, sar,' suggested Sandy. 'I thought the first church-bells came from that direction. Been a lot of gunfire up that way, sar. Good landing-area for troops; sand dunes, firm beaches.'

Stan tried the operator again; she was still sobbing. But she managed to get R N Blyth.

'Garmouth Home Guard here. Blue Flash.' Stan gave the password of the week.

'Hello, old chap. What's all this Blue Flash lark then?' The hair on the back of Stan's neck prickled. Why didn't R N Blyth know the password? The smooth voice at the far end droned on. 'Blue Flash was last week, old son! Password's "Red Sun" this week. It's Sunday night, you know. Password changes 1800 hours Sunday.' The voice spoke perfect English, superior, sneery. Too perfect English? Like Lord Haw-Haw?

Stan shouted, 'I know damn well the password changes 1800 Sunday. Last week's was "Black Stone". This week's is "Blue Flash".'

'Let's have a look. Dear me, old lad, you're quite right. My mistake. It's all this racket outside. Can't hear myself think.'

'Where did "Red Sun" come from, then?' shouted Stan angrily.

'Must be next week's mustn't it?' said the voice, a trifle uneasy now.

'But we're never told next week's till the Wednesday!'

'Weeell ... someone's dropped a clanger then, haven't they, old chap?' The voice was almost a caricature now, sounding falser every minute. A foreigner's idea of a public-school drawl.

'Who are you?' roared Stan. The telephone line suddenly went dead. Stan shuddered. Had he given the code-word to enemy paratroopers?

Mr McGill spoke slowly and clearly down the phone.

'Two houses demolished in Emily Street. Gas main fractured, gas burning, blocking street. Possibly three people trapped in wreckage – at least one still alive. Access by back lane leading from Moreton Street.' He put down the phone, wiping his eyes wearily. When he looked up again, his wife was standing there looking like a ghost.

'Maggie!'

'The bairn's run off somewhere – he ran off when the bells went. I can't find him. Come and help me look.'

'The bairn?' he said steadily. 'Why's the bairn run off?'

Her face crumbled before his eyes; first the mouth began to shake, then her eyes crinkled up, then tears began to stream down her pale cheeks, under the blue headscarf with birds on it. He'd never seen her like this.

Another damage report was slapped in his lap, hurriedly scrawled in indelible pencil on the back of a damp cigarette packet. He picked up the phone to Area HQ again. The report was hard to decipher.

'Boy lying injured in the front garden of 11 Wimbledon Terrace. No, that should be 17 Wimbledon Terrace ... one seven Wimbledon Terrace. Yes, it's off Mendip Road, second on the left going towards the river. Boy cannot be moved – suspected fractured spine. Ambulance essential.' He put down the phone. His wife had collapsed sobbing over the operations table. He shook her by the shoulder timidly.

'Stop it, hinny. It mightn't be him. He might be all right.' She raised a face to him he didn't know – stretched, mad. Her hands reached for his shoulders like claws.

'Come and look. Come and *help* me. *Help* me, *help* me ... I don't know what to *do!*' Mr McGill looked round desperately. His assistants were watching. One had a new damage report in his hand. Mr McGill took it automatically and picked up the phone.

'Outbreak of fire in a warehouse in Dock Road; building contains bales of cloth. No noxious fumes as yet. Fire in danger of spreading to nearby paraffin store. Dock Road blocked by rubble. Access by ...' His wife's shoulders were blocking the access map. He couldn't see where the access route was.

'For God's sake get this woman out of here,' he shouted, as if she was some common stranger. His voice was hard as stone. Two wardens hauled Mrs McGill to her feet.

'Ey, steady up, missus,' said the older one, awkwardly. They half-dragged her to the doorway. She turned and looked at her husband.

'Your own bairn, and you wouldn't look for him. God forgive you, for I never shall.' And she fled sobbing into the night. Mr McGill was seized with a wild urge to run after her, but the phone rang and steadied him.

'Fire engine gone to Dock Road,' he said to his assistants in a whisper. One of the other wardens stuck a red pin in the map. Nobody looked at Mr McGill. He felt very lonely; but quite determined to stay on that phone till the Germans shot it out from under him.

'Time to go, Rudi,' said Clogger. But he really meant time to mend the gun.

Rudi glanced round all the familiar faces; but they were no longer familiar. Clogger held out the greasy cloth with the machine-gun parts wrapped in it.

Rudi hesitated. It was wrong to put such a gun into the hands of children. But what was right tonight? His own people were invading; he had heard the bells. He was confused. These hordes descending on the Blyth beaches, were they friends or foes? These children, preparing to try to kill them, were they foes or friends? Rudi no longer knew; he was muddled. Too weak and muddled to resist the oily cloth thrust at him, the children's air of expectancy.

He bent in the lamplight, and fitted the parts back into the gun. What Clogger had struggled with so many hours was the work of a minute. He cocked the gun and pulled the trigger on an empty breach. It was done.

'So that's how you cock it,' said Chas. 'That's what we did wrong. We forgot to re-cock it.' His voice sounded glad, excited. 'Now who'll take Rudi to the boat?'

'I will,' said Nicky. Everyone shook hands quickly; nobody looked at anybody else. Nicky's and Rudi's footsteps faded into the night. The silence was awful.

'Let's sing, quietly,' said Audrey. The song they sang

was *Ich hatt' einen kameraden* and a lot of tears were surreptitiously flicked from faces.

The telephone from Number Two post rang. Everybody on the roof of Billing's Mill jumped.

'Sergeant Watson here, sir.'

'Yes?'

'Do we search everyone who passes us, sir? There's a terrible lot of people on the road, walking with bundles. Heading towards Newcastle, most of them.'

'Yes, stop and search everybody. Try and turn them back if you can. They'll only block the roads and spread panic. We don't want it like France, do we?'

'Righto, sir.'

Stan hung up and rubbed his bristled cheeks. They felt stiff and painful. Three hours they had been waiting, and still no definite word of the invasion, one way or the other. The telephone exchange had stopped answering altogether. Hit by a bomb, captured by the enemy, or just choked with calls?

'What about us taking the van and running down to the Castle, sarnt-major? They might know something definite.'

'I'd like to, sar, only well ... aren't there enough folk flying round like paper kites already? I think we'd do better just sitting tight and doing our job. Something might happen at one of our posts the moment we turned our backs, sar. That's the hardest part of any battle, sar – sitting and waiting; with respect, sar.' Sandy clicked his heels together.

'Carry on, then, sarnt-major,' said Stan. God bless you, Sandy, he thought. God bless your simple heart.

'Mullins here, sir. Jerry's come, sir. At least I think he has. Can you come quick with all the lads you've got, sir.'

They got the twelve men of the reserve into the tiny van somehow, with a desperate clatter of rifles. Stan drove, thinking about Number One point. It was a good solid concrete pillbox. 'A' platoon, which held it, was the strongest platoon – thirty two men with old Canadian rifles, and an ancient Lewis machine-gun, the pride of the company. With fourteen extra, we can make some kind of show, thought Stan. But why can't I hear any firing?

They pulled up by the silent pillbox with a squeal of brakes. Mullins was waiting. The men leapt out quickly, and took shelter behind the pillbox, glancing round the corners nervously.

'Which way are they, Mullins?'

'On the road, sir, beyond the bridge. In lorries they are, sir, about two or three hundred strong. Ten lorries and a command-car, anyway. They've got out and are lounging about. Mr Whiteload's talking to the fellow who seems to be in charge.'

'Talking?'

'They're trying to bluff their way through, I reckon. They can't know how little we've got inside this pillbox, can they?'

'And they're coming from the direction of Newcastle, *towards* the coast?'

'Part of their bluff, sir. Isn't that what you'd do?'

'How do you know they're Germans?'

'They're foreigners for sure – you should hear 'em babble. And they haven't got no movement order. Mr Whiteload asked them for that, straight away.'

All the while, Stan, Sandy and the sergeant had been walking across the bridge to the trucks.

'British Army trucks,' said Stan.

'They captured plenty at Dunkirk, sar,' said Sandy.

'British uniforms,' said Stan.

'But they're not wearing them British-style,' said Sandy. 'Too sloppy. No backbone.'

Two figures stood in the middle of the road, arguing violently. One was Mr Whiteload. The other ... well ... he certainly wasn't British. A heavy black moustache swooped to the corners of his mouth. Eyebrows, equally heavy, drooped to high cheekbones. His accent was heavy, and his gestures dramatic.

'I'm glad you've come, sir,' said Whiteload, a bespectacled ex-public schoolboy with flat feet. 'This officer says he is Major er ... er ...'

'Koslowski. Stanislaus Koslowski, Major, Polish Free Army, at your service.' His jackboots clicked loudly together. The salute was like something in the movies, the handshake like a bear's. 'I am bloody-marvellously amazed to make your acquaintance, Colonel.'

'What are you chaps doing on the move without a movement order?'

'Ve no vait for any bloody movement order. Germans come – is enough: We go kill bloody Germans. Do ve need a killing-Germans-order also? Poles can kill Nazis without orders.'

'Look, old lad. If everyone goes off half-cock without orders we shall have chaos.'

'Ho yes, Englishman. You want everything nice and neat, like your bloody privet hedges, like your wife's kitchen at home. My wife not at home. Wife and children is dead, road out of Warsaw. Nazi fighter shoots them into very small bits. Not neat, eh?'

'I'm *sorry,*' said Stan, getting cross. But he was really starting to wonder if this *could* possibly be the hyper-efficient German Wehrmacht.

'I take you to my general,' announced the moustached man, dragging Stan in a bear-like hug down the road

168

'General Prince Gerard Nowicki.' Stan didn't even try to struggle – it would be too undignified.

General Prince Nowicki, standing in the pale moonlight, was like a figure out of a musical-comedy: with a four-cornered peaked cap, riding cape and pale aristocratic profile. The man stood only five feet tall, and must be seventy if he was a day.

'My dear Captain ... Liddell. And you are of the British Home Guard, I see. And you hold this bridge most stubbornly, even against your allies.' Stan felt ashamed. The Germans could *never* have invented *him*.

'How can we settle our differences, Captain? Let us go to your HQ, and leave our stout fellows here to guard each other. I shall make sure mine do not open fire first ...' He called out orders in a foreign language, not loud but silvery, so they carried, over the noises of that night.

'Let us drive to your HQ in comfort, in my car, Captain.'

'Stand fast, Mr Whiteload,' muttered Stan, as he was led away. He felt outwitted, somehow.

Fatty Hardy had the situation well in hand. The main problem was to stop German parachutists and saboteurs getting down Saville Street. After all, it was the main street of Garmouth. It hardly occurred to him that saboteurs might prefer to sneak down back lanes. Anyway, he couldn't be responsible for *everything*.

So it was there he made his stand. He requisitioned three passing special constables to help him, and luckily one had a car. With a car, they blocked Saville Street, leaving only a three-foot space to get past. In this space, Fatty set a table and chair from a bombed house, and on the chair he placed his own ample bottom. The light from a nearby burning house gave enough light to read people's identity-cards. Then two soldiers home on leave turned up with their rifles. Really, thought Fatty, it was the perfect set-up.

It was. A queue of refugees rapidly formed. Three fire engines on their way to fires were unable to get past because their crews couldn't produce identity-cards. They departed with such streams of language as German saboteurs could never have achieved.

It was just after this that Rudi and Nicky ran round the corner, and slap into the queue. In fact, they tried to hurry past before they realized it was a queue.

'Ey, get in line there. Who do you think you are?' growled a big man carrying a clothes basket full of blankets and tinned food. Everyone turned and stared at them. They retired to the end of the queue.

'Let's run,' whispered Nicky. Rudi took the child's hand. It was as cold as ice and shaking violently.

'Let's walk,' said Rudi. He managed to keep calm for the boy's sake.

But when they turned away, a soldier with a fixed bayonet turned them back.

'Get in the queue, you! If you've got nowt to hide, you've got nowt to fear.' He waved his bayonet in their faces; he was wild with fright like everyone else.

Fatty Hardy made a fuss about everybody, as they came up to his table. Identity cards were not enough. They had to turn out their bundles, say where they were going. People swore at him, and he swore back. It got tenser and tenser. And the queue in front of Rudi and Nicky got shorter and shorter.

'What shall we do?' whispered Nicky.

'There nothing is we can do. Those soldiers they will shoot us if we run. Only thing to do is for you to leave go of my hand. On your own, you are safe. Be sensible, *hein*?'

But Nicky clung to Rudi's hand all the tighter.

170

Then it was their turn at the table.

'Identity cards?' Rudi's tongue clove to his mouth.

'Hurry up. Identity cards.' Fatty Hardy squinted up at them. He was sweating. Rudi felt Nicky take a huge breath.

'We ain't got none,' said Nicky. He spoke like a ragamuffin. In his tattered balaclava helmet, even his own schoolmates wouldn't have recognized him.

'Shut up, kid. I'm talking to your dad.'

'Me dad's deaf and dumb.' Nicky clutched Rudi's hand tighter still. 'We're going to see if me gran's all right.'

'What's your name?'

'Webster.'

'Where d'you live?'

'Simon Street.'

'But Simon Street's down there.' Fatty Hardy jerked his thumb towards the silent road beyond the barrier. Rudi felt Nicky catch his breath.

'No, it's me gran lives in Simon Street.'

Fatty Hardy glared at Rudi hard. 'I never heard of no dumbie down Simon Street, and I only live three streets away. Hey, there's something fishy here. What you two up to?' The two soldiers, hearing the urgency in the policeman's voice, closed up with their bayonets. Rudi closed his eyes.

And then there was a faint shout of 'Help'. Everyone turned. A huge figure was approaching, running with flailing arms and wide open mouth. A little woman ran close behind.

'It's John,' gasped Nicky. The flailing figure ran straight through the queue, scattering people like nine-pins. It crashed into the car's bonnet with a whoosh of breath.

'Grab him!' shouted Fatty Hardy. Two special constables leapt in and grabbed John's arms. He bellowed like

171

a bull and threw them off. Then he threw over the table at which Fatty Hardy was sitting. Hardy grabbed at him, men ran to help, and the table collapsed under a scrum of struggling bodies.

One man leapt out with a bleeding ear.

'He bit me, the Nazi swine!' Mrs Brownlee stood wringing her hands.

'Oh, please don't hurt him. He's gentle as a lamb – don't frighten him.'

At last, they hauled John to his feet, and Fatty Hardy slipped a pair of handcuffs on him.

'Oh, please, he's not a Nazi,' wailed Mrs Brownlee, 'he's just our John.' Fatty Hardy looked at the heaving gibbering figure.

'Where you going now?' said John. 'Where you going now?'

'By heck, it *is* that idiot from the Square. He's gone nuts. Loony Bin for him, missus. Straight away. Get him in the car.'

'Oh, no, please. I can handle him. He's quiet as a lamb usually.'

'Tell that to the doctor at Morpeth, missus.'

Rudi felt a tug at his hand.

'*C'mon*,' muttered Nicky.

Nobody noticed them go.

Nicky swung back the river-door of the boathouse.

'Use your oars till you get clear of the Castle Cliff,' he said, 'and then pull on this rope to raise the big sail. The little one's more complicated, but it's not so important.'

'Right,' said Rudi, clambering down into the dinghy. It rocked alarmingly to his landlubber's feet. He settled down and unshipped the oars.

'Thanks a lot, Nicky. A clever trick it was, telling the

172

polizei I was your deaf and dumb dad. I thought I a dead man was.'

'Rudi?'

'*Ja?*'

'I wish you were my dad. Can't I come with you?' Rudi could hear the tears in his voice.

'*Nein.* Where I go, no place for you is.'

'I could sail the boat for you. I'm an expert, honest. Only ... the boat's going, and you're going ... and there's nothing left.'

'*Nein, liebling.* There is much left; your *kamerads,* your gun, your country.'

'But I like you better. Better even than my father.'

'And I you. But we both our duties have. Perhaps I see you after the War. Then we all *kamerads* be, *hein?*' The boy began to cry uncontrollably. There was nothing to do but push off into the night, leaving the sobs to dwindle.

The moon was very bright, the rowlocks noisy, and the guardship on the boom very near. Rudi found the oars hard to manage; the boat kept on turning towards the guardship.

They must see me soon, Rudi thought.

But overhead a fresh wave of bombers roared in. The AA guns roared, and every eye on the guardship turned skyward. Rudi looked up at the black planes with their tiny wing-crosses, twisting and bouncing in the searchlight beams.

'Poor bastards!'

Then he looked at the burning docks and repeated, 'Poor bastards!' War seemed very stupid, but he rowed on, trying to be a hero. There was nothing else to do.

As soon as he rounded Castle Cliff, he felt the wind. He raised the sail and headed north-east. If there was an invasion, that was where the German fleet would be lying.

The night-breeze filled the sail, and the water chuckled under the bow and stern.

At the Mill, the General Prince graciously took a chair, neatly crossing his tiny riding boots, while Stan got put through to Northern Command HQ at York.

'Northern Command. General Wilberforce's staff,' said a voice in lazy Oxford English.

'Garmouth Home Guard here. Blue Flash.'

'Yes, OK, Blue Flash. Fire away.' Stan explained his problem. The languid voice on the far end groaned.

'Oh, God, not Nowicki's lot *again*! A little fellow with a comic-opera fancy-dress? Oh, yes, they're Polish Army all right, and don't I know it; what have they been up to *now*?'

Stan told him.

'But there isn't any German invasion. Every radar-screen's been clear all night. Some short-circuit in a police telephone box at Blyth started the bell ringing and it's all snowballed from there. God, what a bloody fuss about nothing. Tell Nowicki to pack up and go home; he's wasting petrol.'

'*You* tell him,' said Stan. Now it was all over he felt unbearably weary.

'Put him on then,' General Nowicki listened, head cocked like a bird.

'Ah so! But I will just go and look for myself round Blyth. Better is safe than sorry.'

'That's the last of your month's petrol ration,' quacked the voice on the phone piercingly.

'If German come we find more, no?' Norwicki put the phone down with a cherubic smile. 'In Blyth we for Germans will look. But a drink to you and your brave chaps before we go, Captain Siddall.'

174

'Liddell,' said Stan. The General Prince produced a flask and two glasses. The drink burnt Stan's mouth like flame. He was vaguely aware that the Prince smashed his glass into the fireplace and was gone. With a throat like a nutmeg-grater, Stan picked up Number One phone and told Sergeant Mullins the convoy could go through.

Rudi came awake with a start, and he was still in the dark in his little boat. He must have dozed off. It had got so peaceful; peaceful and cold.

He looked back towards the shore; the guns had stopped, the bombing had stopped. The pink fires over the Gar were dying down. In the other direction, where the German invasion fleet should be lying off Blyth, there was simply darkness.

Suddenly Rudi *knew* there was no invasion. His nearest fellow-German was three hundred miles away. It had all been British hysteria. He was more alone than he had ever been. He held on towards Germany for half-an-hour, while his feet and hands turned slowly numb.

Finally, he swore, swung over the tiller and reversed course back to Garmouth. Cold heroism was not in him. He was going home to the Fortress.

SEVENTEEN

In Garmouth, the hysteria died as the bombing died. The truth of no invasion spread as quickly as the false rumour had done.

It was suddenly a working Monday morning, and raining.

Fatty Hardy puffed indignantly to himself as he pedalled his bike up the Blyth Road. As if false invasions weren't enough, four silly kids had to go missing. Four sets of panicking parents were raising hell at the police-station. Fatty had been told the kids' names over the phone, but he hadn't really listened. What he had grasped was that he had been given the Heath to search, right down to the sea; a square mile of dense grass, all on his own. After being up all night. He'd not get home till tea-time.

Hallo, what was this? Soldiers? Lots of soldiers in lorries. Ahah! If he could persuade them into helping he could be home for breakfast in an hour. He held up the authoritative arm of the law.

The convoy ground to a halt. A heavily moustached face peered out of the leading car.

'Constable – the best of good mornings. How am I bloody able to help you?'

Foreign soldiers? Fatty glanced at the man's shoulder flash. Ah, the Polish Corps – the Polskis. Well, better than nothing. They had two eyes each, anyway. He explained.

'Ah yes, helping we most certainly will. We form a line down to the beach, huh, and sweeps towards that bombed house, huh? Yes, my men could doings with a walk. They are cooped up all night. We find no Jerries nowhere. I tell General Prince Nowicki and we are starting.'

The Poles fanned out rapidly. They carried their weapons from habit. They started. Far off, across the Heath, the Nicholl house rose from its necklace of winter trees.

Chas came to with a gasp, his chin resting on the rough weave of the sandbags. At first he was ashamed at having fallen asleep, but then he saw all the others had fallen asleep too. He was as stiff as an old horse; his tummy rumbled loudly. Like the others, he had spent half the night eating anything he could lay his hands on. Eating and swallowing stopped you feeling sick all the time.

What had they talked about? What it was like to be hurt; what it was like to be dead. There had been a stupid argument about God, which had ended in Nicky attacking Cem, and the usually calm Cem fighting back viciously. Audrey had declaimed the Agincourt speech from *Henry V* which she had learned by heart, and everyone had yelled it was stupid rubbish, and then *she* had burst into tears. What an awful stupid night.

He looked out of the firing-slit. Everything was still, silent. The world felt totally empty.

Where are the Germans? he thought. God, has everyone run away and left us?

It was the dawn of a new day, though not a bright one. Mist lay thick on the grass of the Heath, all the way down to the sea.

And then Chas moaned. Out of the mist lines of soldiers were walking. Their uniforms looked grey, and they called to each other in a harsh foreign language. Hundreds and hundreds of them!

'Clogger! Carrots! Wake up, they've come. Jerry's here.'

177

They leapt into life, hearts thumping like engines. Clogger grabbed the Luger, and leapt out into the trench. Cem grabbed the air-rifle, and leapt the other way. Nick grabbed the magazine for the gun.

'Load!' yelled Chas. 'Cock. Range?'

'They're aye up tey the white fence,' shouted Clogger.

'That's three-fifty yards.'

'Three hundred.'

'Go on,' said Chas. 'I've paced it a dozen times.'

'Yer puny pace is no a yard,' said Clogger firmly.

''Tis so.' And Chas set the sight firmly at three hundred and fifty. He never realized the Germans used metres. He lay down and put his eye carefully to the sight, wriggling his shoulders to get comfortable. He watched the first man come up to the fence.

'Hey, Fatty Hardy's with them. Pointing things out to them.'

'He's a Quisling!' shouted Clogger.

'Perhaps he's their prisoner.'

'We can't help that. Fire before they're right on top of us!'

The gun roared and slammed in Chas's hands. When the smoke cleared away, there wasn't a man to be seen. I can't have killed them all, he thought.

And then, all along the ground where the Germans had been came little winking flashes of fire.

Fatty Hardy felt bemused. One minute he had been walking along feeling very important; the next, he was lying face down in a muddy little stream, where someone had pushed him.

'Ey, what's the game?' he spluttered, starting up. A brawny Polish arm knocked him down again.

'Keepings down. Germans.' Another flight of bullets

178

sang overhead. Then the Poles were firing back, a tremendous booming din. Sand and rock-splinters spouted from the area in front of the Nichol house. Under cover of the fire, groups of Poles were crawling forward at amazing speed, cradling their rifles between their flailing elbows.

'Ey, stop that shooting,' said Fatty Hardy. 'You'll kill somebody!'

'That is our work, killing Nazis,' said Major Koslowski placidly.

'But there ain't no Germans.'

'What are these shooting at us then – Boy Scouts? Is paratroopers landed.' The Major shouted further orders. Another flight of bullets passed overhead. 'The Nazi fools are shootings too high. Soon we have them. One hand-grenade and ... pouf!'

Then, abruptly the firing stopped. Hardy looked up. A scarecrow figure, waving a dirty white flag on a twig, was walking out from between the trees right in front of where the enemy machine-gun lay.

'Ah, see, typical Nazis – cowards and improperly dressed too. I have a mind to shoot him as a spy.'

'You can't shoot a man who's carrying a white flag,' spluttered Fatty Harding. 'It's not fair.'

'Ah, the English gentleman – always so bloody fair. Perhaps if your homes had been burnt to the ground you would not be so concerned to be bloody fair.'

The scarecrow figure reached the first Poles. They searched him for weapons and frogmarched him back to the major, arms twisted cruelly behind his back. From a doubled-up position he gasped.

'Rudi Gerlath, Sergeant, Luftwaffe, 764532.'

'Spy,' shouted the Major. 'You will be shot, and all the others with you.'

'There no others are. Back there is children.'

'*Children*?'

'*Ja* – six schoolkids.'

Light dawned on Fatty Hardy. 'Is one called McGill?'

'*Ja* – Chassy McGill.'

Fatty Hardy wiped the dribbles of water off his face; he adjusted his helmet and his most fearsome expression. Suddenly, he knew where he was.

'McGill. I might have known it!'

EIGHTEEN

CHAS sat helpless. There wasn't a German in sight, except Rudi. Rudi was talking to Fatty Hardy. Then it all got very muddling.

A police-car turned up, disgorging the sergeant with the limp, and two more constables. Then a van turned up, and disgorged Mr Liddell and ten Home Guard.

'Are they all Quislings?' wailed Cem in wonder. Then all the German soldiers got up in a very relaxed sort of way, and began trailing away, smoking cigarettes. He couldn't fire at them for fear of hitting the English people. Somehow he couldn't shoot Stan Liddell, even if he was a Quisling. Then more cars arrived. His mother and father got out and Mr and Mrs Parton ...

'Cor, there's me dad,' said Carrot-juice.

'And mine,' said Cem Jones. 'Hey, do you think the Germans are using them as hostages?'

'Dunno,' said Chas abruptly, as if he were brushing off a fly. For the Germans were retreating all the way to the skyline, and getting into trucks. The mist was clearing from the landscape now; but Chas felt it was settling into his mind instead. The Germans drove away.

Then all the police and parents began advancing on the Fortress. They didn't look scared, as hostages should. They just looked very angry. Chas saw his father's fists were clenched.

'Oh, God, what have we *done*?' wailed Cem.

The world had two faces. Which was the true one? The world of the long night of waiting, of Stukas and Panzers, stormtroopers and death? Or the world of day, of punishments, hidings and magistrate's court? They couldn't decide. And the advancing horde gave them no time to decide.

Something broke inside the children. The Luger cracked once, and the bullet whined wildly into the sky. As one, police, parents and Home Guard flung themselves on to their faces. They looked pathetic, ridiculous and hateful lying there.

'Go back, sod off. Leave us alone,' screamed Chas. 'Sod off or we'll *shoot*.' Suddenly, he hated them all. He went on and on shouting. 'Go away! Go away! Sod off, you bastards. Leave us *alone*!' The parents did not move.

Then Rudi, alone, got to his feet and began walking towards them.

'Get back, Rudi, get back.'

Rudi went on advancing, blocking off the field of fire of the gun. The children could no longer see what was happening behind him, and they *had* to know.

'Oh, God!' said Clogger, and fired the Luger. Rudi smiled stupidly, raised one hand towards them, and fell to the ground.

'Oh, *Rudi*!' cried Audrey, and ran out to him. In a second, all the children were gathered round him. He was lying on his back, pale and trying to speak, with a red stain spreading across his grey flying-jacket.

The ambulance had gone. The children stood in one huddled group, the adults in another. Shock still froze every face, but on the faces of the adults it was beginning to melt into righteous anger. The police sergeant fingered his notebook impatiently; Mr McGill fingered the buckle of his belt; Mr Parton's voice was raised in a querulous demand to know what things were coming to. All the adults were already busy, tidying up things in their minds, making them into more comfortable shapes.

'I don't know what's got into him!'

'Wait till I get *her* home!'

'Hooliganism!'

Stan Liddell made his mind up. If being Home Guard Commander had its responsibilities, it also had its privileges.

'Clear the area,' he said to his men. Then he said it sharper. 'Clear the *area*. This is a military *matter*.' The Home Guard began to push the parents away apologetically, with their rifles. Sandy finished off the job with a *look*.

'That means you, Constable, and you too, Sergeant. You put this matter in my hands and I'm keeping it there for the moment. Your time will come.' The lame police sergeant flinched. Stan felt a pang of regret, but the children would never tell the truth with that peevish face around. Both policemen walked away, backs stiff with rage.

'Now how about showing us ... all this, McGill, will you?'

The children led him and Sandy inside. They answered every question with mono-syllables, and shut faces. Only when Sandy boomed, 'This is a good 'ole. A very good 'ole indeed! Well made to last. I could 'ave done with this 'ole in the Somme in 1917,' did their faces break into peaked grins that vanished as soon as they appeared. Stan left it to Sandy. The kids were obviously warming to him.

'I'd like to take this whole thing over, sar, for the 'Ome Guard. We 'aven't got nothing as good as this.'

What was the sarnt-major talking about? The dugout was well-made enough, but totally in the wrong place. It defended nothing. Then he looked at the children's faces and understood. That brief smile was back again.

'And will you hand over your weapons please, lady and gentlemen? We 'aven't got nothing as good as that machine-gun.'

Chas nodded. He picked up the Luger and put it into Sandy's giant fist.

'I dare say they can come up to the Mill sometimes, sar, and see the guns?' Stan nodded.

'Cem and I will come,' Chas said, 'if we're not sent away to a school. These two can't.' He indicated Clogger and Nicky. 'They'll have to go into a home.'

Stan wanted to say he'd see it didn't happen. But he couldn't see it didn't happen. He couldn't even promise that Chas and Cem wouldn't be sent to an approved school. He looked at Chas.

'Will you tell me how it all started?'

Chas looked at him.

'No, sir. You'd never understand. Grown-ups never do.'

'Is there any way I *can* help?'

'Can you get Clogger and Nicky into the same home? Nicky needs Clogger.'

'I'll try.'

'And can you get permission for us to write to Rudi if . . . if . . . And let us know how he gets on?'

Every child's face softened. Lucky Rudi, thought Stan. Lucky enemy. If he lived.

'I can certainly do that.'

'Thank you.'

'Can we have a minute together, sir? Alone?'

As Stan emerged from the dugout, Mr Parton came storming up to him.

'This is outrageous, Mr Liddell. Why can't we see our children? I shall complain to the Education Committee about this.'

'I am not acting under the orders of the Education Committee. I am acting under the authority of Northern Command, York. Kindly address your complaints to the

184

Brigadier there.' Stan's voice was cutting and very precise. 'And Mr Parton?'

'Yes?'

'Where were you going in your car when my men turned you back on the Coast Road Bridge last night?'

'On a visit to my sister in the Lake District – we go every spring.'

'In the middle of the night?'

'Yes.'

'Leaving your daughter behind?'

'That's none of your business.'

'But where did you get the petrol?' Stan turned to the police sergeant viciously. '*There's* a case for you, Sergeant. Black Market. I look forward to seeing it reported in the local newspaper. In *full* detail.'

'What are you looking at me like that for, Mr McGill,' said Mr Parton petulantly.

'I'll not say *much* for my lad,' said Mr McGill slowly, 'except he thought he was *fighting* the Germans.'

'Oh, hush,' said Mrs McGill. 'Chassy could have killed somebody.'

'I'm not talking about his sense, missus. I'm talking about his guts.'

'Aye,' said Cem Senior, looking hard at Mr Parton. 'That's one thing the kids didn't lack. Guts.' And he spat on the ground.

'Cheeroh,' said Chas to Clogger, suddenly.

'Cheeroh, boy,' said Clogger. 'Nil carborundum. Don't let the bastards grind ye down.'

'Write to me. I'll let you know about Rudi.'

'Aye, mevve. If they'll let me.' Then he grinned because he remembered Chas, wreathed in smoke from the gun, standing swearing blue murder and quite unafraid, while

185

Polish bullets hammered into the sandbags all around him.

'Ye're a hard man, Chassy McGill. It was a bonny fight. Mevve we'll be in the real one, before it's over.'

'I hope so,' said Chas, and went round the gang for the last time, shaking hands, looking at faces.

'G'bye, Nicky.'

'Nil carborundum,' said Nicky faintly, trying hard not to cry and managing it.

'G'bye, Cem. See you in court.' Cem laughed, his old ridiculous laugh.

'G'bye, Audrey. You were as good as any boy.'

'Thanks,' said Audrey.

'G'bye, Carrot-juice.'

'Thanks for letting me in on it. It was great.'

So they parted, never to be all together again. They walked across to their parents. Their arms were grabbed roughly, and they were led away.

'You're not to play with that McGill again,' said Mrs Jones in a savage whisper.

'That Cemetery Jones always got you into trouble,' said Mrs McGill. 'You've nigh broken your dad's heart.'

'You're not to play with those big rough boys. You know you're easy led astray,' said Carrot-juice's dad.

'I don't know *what* got into you,' said Mr Parton. 'You'll stay home at nights in future. I'll make a lady of you if it kills you.'

'You're too much for me,' said Clogger's aunt. 'I'm having you put away.'

'C'mon son,' said the police sergeant to Nicky. 'You're going to tell me all about this. You're a cut above the rest of this riff-raff, you know. *Your* father was a ship's captain. God knows what he'd have said.'

Nicky took a deep breath.

'Get stuffed,' he said.

186

Also in *M Books*

The Pigman Paul Zindel
They swear an oath: 'Let it be known that Lorraine Jensen and
John Conlan have decided to record the facts, and only the
facts, about our experiences with Mr Angelo Pignati'. They
befriend Mr Pignati – the Pigman because he collects piggy-
banks – almost as a joke. He, a lonely old man whose wife has
died, welcomes their friendship and allows them the run of his
home. Which is when the trouble starts, for John and Lorraine
have yet to discover the power of resentment and selfishness,
jealousy and rivalry as well as of love and self-respect. Mr
Pignati dies before they discover the truth.
ISBN 0 333 24087 1

The Outsiders S. E. Hinton
Greasers, rockers – different places, different names; but
whatever they are, they're the outsiders. The rough, tough,
long-haired boys from the 'other' side of town. They have little
hope of owning Mustang cars, madras shirts or any of the
good things of American life. This is their story, told by
Ponyboy, a greaser with good reason to fear the Socs (the lucky
boys who drive Mustangs) and a witness to the savage baiting
which leads his best friend to manslaughter. But this is more
than a story of the warfare between the greasers and the Socs.
It is also a story of loyalty and affection among friends, and of
the fumbling search by teenagers of the urban slums for
personal dignity and a place in the world.
ISBN 0 333 24319 6

Fireweed Jill Paton Walsh
London, 1940. The Blitz. Almost nightly, German bombers
rain destruction on the city. Like hundreds of others, two
young people, Bill and Julie, set up a make-shift home among
the ruins where soon only fireweed will grow. They survive as
best they can, keeping out of sight of the authorities who want
to evacuate them to the safety of the countryside. Thrown
together by circumstances, they discover the things that make
life worth living and the evils that set people apart.
ISBN 0 333 24779 5

I Never Loved Your Mind Paul Zindel

When Dewey Daniels saw Yvette Goethals for the first time, the thought crossed his mind that she might be an adolescent ghoul. She had a chalk-white face framed by dark-brown hair which hung down like dried vermicelli. But she did have a nice sort of smile every once in a while, and Dewey wondered if they might have something in common because they had both dropped out of school.

It turns out they do have things in common, and soon they are enjoying life together. But Yvette is an idealist, and is exploring alternatives to the society she sees around her every day and which she doesn't like. She takes Dewey along with her as she explores. She also wants to find out whether she loves his mind as much as she loves his body.

A story of two bright, zany drop-outs who can't find what they want together but can't stop trying to discover it either because they know it is important to get the world right.
ISBN 0 333 27869 0

Mr Corbett's Ghost Leon Garfield

New Year's Eve: 'A windy night and the old year dying of an ague.' Benjamin Partridge, in the depths of despair, wishes his master, Mr Corbett, dead and in the grave... And tonight, on the bleak heights of Hampstead Heath, his wish is granted... Mr Corbett's ghost rises from his lifeless body, and Benjamin Partridge finds himself faced with emotions and events for which he had not bargained.

Vaarlem and Tripp and *The Simpleton* make up this threesome of stories which tease the mind and entertain with their imaginative plots and colourful characters.
ISBN 0 333 27862 3

I Am David Anne Holm

David has known no other life than that of the concentration camp. Then he is allowed to escape. Reserved and watchful, he wanders through Europe, fearful that *They* will catch him, mistrustful of everyone he meets. This world outside the camp is so strange to him he does not even know what things are good to eat and what bad. Only gradually on his long and dangerous journey does he lose his fear and mistrust and learn why he was allowed to escape.
ISBN 0 333 24487 7

The Day of the Pigeons Roy Brown

Mousy Lawson runs away from Approved School one Friday
evening. He is determined to find his father who has just
written saying he has married again and is leaving the country.
Mousy gets a lift in a lorry, reaches London, finds an empty
basement in which to live, and starts looking for his
father. That's when Chris enters Mousy's life, in search of
Monsieur Poirot's prize pigeons. Unwillingly Chris is dragged
into Mousy's search and it is not long before he is unsure what
to do about Mousy – or Mousy's criminal father.

ISBN 0 333 25715 4

That Was Then, This Is Now S.E. Hinton

From the time they were children, they had been best friends,
like brothers. Now, at sixteen, they are still inseparable, even
though Bryon spends a lot of time chatting up the girls, and
likes hustling for money in Charlie's Bar.

And then Charlie gets shot – killed – trying to protect Bryon
and Mark from getting beaten up in the alley. Mark called it
fate. After all, they were still kids really. But then M & M, their
pal and the brother of Cathy, Bryon's special girl, disappears.
When Bryon discovers what has happened to M & M he knows
he has to make a terrible decision. They are kids no more; that
was then, this is now. And what he must do now means the
end of childhood and, maybe the end of a long friendship.

ISBN 0 333 27863 1

Time Trap Nicholas Fisk

The year is 2079. Most of the earth is a poisoned wasteland.
People live in Homebody Units and spend their time watching
the Viddy screen. But Dano rebels against this mindless
existence. He is befriended by the eccentric Uncle Lipton, a
failed galactic pilot, who is more than 130 years old and still
going strong, thanks to the secret life-prolonging drug Xtend,
which also enables him to travel in time. Thinking he can
escape the present, Dano agrees to travel with Uncle Lipton.
But the drug's time-travel effects are only temporary. At the
moment he sees his own terrifying future, he realises the drug
cannot help him.

ISBN 0 333 24318 8

The Chocolate War Robert Cormier

Even the calm, corrupt Archie Costello, leader of The Vigils, that most dreaded of school secret societies, has to admit that twenty thousand boxes of chocolates will take some selling. But one does not refuse an appeal from Brother Leon, for whose ambition and lack of moral scuple Archie has a shrewd respect.

Brother Leon is organising the school's annual fund-raising effort, by tradition a sale of chocolates. He is also the form master of Jerry Renault, new boy, honest, straightforward – 'square' they call him – with a mother just dead and a father on whome he has learned not to depend. It is Jerry whom Archie selects as his victim: public victimisation is the deadly weapon chosen by the leader of The Vigils as the surest way to win the Chocolate War. But even Archie has underestimated the hidden strength of his victim.

ISBN 0 333 24316 1

The Slave Dancer Paula Fox

The crew of a slave ship was never very large: the fewer the better when the money was shared out. Why had Jessie Bollier been captured from a New Orleans backstreet, loitering on his way home to his mother with Aunt Agatha's candle stubs? He learnt the answers on the long voyage to Africa, learnt too something of the nature of the men he so unwillingly sailed with: Ned Grime, Ben Stout, Nicholas Spark the mate, Purvis the sailmaker and Captain Cawthorne. However, nothing prepared him for the reality of a cargo of Black Gold or for his own hideous task: playing the fife to 'dance the slaves'.

ISBN 0 333 26008 2

Published by Thomas Nelson and Sons Ltd